The Art of

MACHINE PIECING

Sally Collins

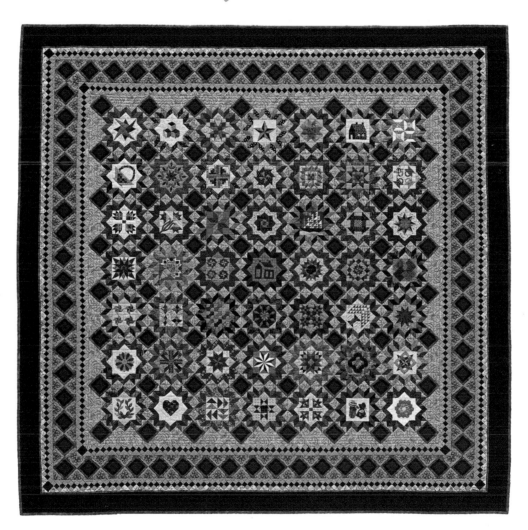

How to Achieve Quality Workmanship

Through a Colorful Journey

C&T PUBLISHING

Copyright © 2001 Sally Collins
Editor: Beate Marie Nellemann
Technical Editor: Joyce Engels Lytle
Quilt Photography: Sharon Risedorph
Illustrations: Aliza Kahn © C&T Publishing
How-to Photography: Stephen Fridge
Production Assistants: Stacy Chamness, Claudia Böhm
Book Design: Nancy Koerner
Front and Back Cover: *My Journey.* Made by Sally Collins
Design Direction: Diane Pedersen
Cover Design: Kristen Yenche

Library of Congress Cataloging-in-Publication Data

Collins, Sally
   The art of machine piecing : how to achieve quality workmanship through a colorful journey / Sally Collins.
         p.   cm.
Includes bibliographical references and index.
   ISBN 1-57120-119-X (pbk.)
   1. Quilting—Patterns. 2. Patchwork—Patterns. 3. Machine quilting. I. Title.
   TT835 .C647396 2001
   746.46'041—dc21

                    00-010840

We have made every attempt to properly credit the trademark and brand names of the items mentioned in this book. We apologize to any companies that have been listed incorrectly, and we would appreciate hearing from you.

Bias Bars is a trademark of Celtic Design Co.
C-Thru Ruler is a registered trademark of C-Thru Ruler Co.
DMC is a registered trademark of DMC Corporation.
Exacto is a registered trademark of Hunt Manufacturing Company.
Glue-Baste-It is a trademark of Roxanne's International, Inc.
Hot Tape is a trademark of Distlefink Designs, Inc.
Masonite is a trademark of Masonite Corp.
Omnigrid is registered trademark of Omnigrid, Inc.
Pfaff is a registered trademark of Pfaff Corp.
Quilters' GluTube is a registered trademark manufactured
   by Mark-Tex. exclusively for Quilting Techniques, Inc.
Schmetz is a brand name of Ferdinand Schmetz, GmbH., Germany.

Permission has graciously been given by Jinny Beyer to share her block California Sunset, page 94, from her book, *Quilters Album of Blocks and Borders*, 1980; Judy Martin to share her blocks, Vagabond, page 93, and Mississippi Queen, page 56, from her book, *Ultimate Book of Quilt Block Patterns*, 1988, Charleston Quilt, page 103, and Carnival Ride, page 96, from her book, *Scraps, Blocks and Quilts*, 1990; Elly Sienkiewicz to share her block, Ruched Rose Lyre (Heart and Leaf Lyre), page 82, from her book, *Baltimore Beauties and Beyond*, 2000.

Published by C & T Publishing, Inc.
P.O. Box 1456
Lafayette, California 94549

Printed in Singapore
10 9 8 7 6 5 4 3 2

Table of Contents

Acknowledgments

The following deserve my special thanks for their love, support and encouragement. This book would not exist without their help.

Thank you, C & T Publishing, for the faith and encouragement to transform an idea into reality.

Thank you, Joyce Lytle, Beate Nellemann, Stacy Chamness, and Diane Pedersen, for your caring advice and expert editing.

Thank you, my students, for encouragement and inspiration to explore, improve and teach.

Thank you, Kathleen Pappas, for your input and computer wizardry.

Thank you, my Joe, for loving me unconditionally, sharing my passion for quality without compromise, and for living a truly wonderful life!

Dedication

This book is dedicated to Chuck Tear, my Dad, the person who taught me by example the values that come from doing ones best and reaching for only the best.

Thank you, Dad; I love you with all my heart.

Preface

I will be forever grateful for my introduction to quiltmaking. It was a process that began with drafting basic blocks and making templates without the use of a rotary cutter. My appreciation for the technical process and my attention for accuracy and quality workmanship began in those early exercises.

I was drawn to smaller blocks (usually 3" squares), which at first challenged and later helped improve my drafting and sewing abilities. As is usual with all learning, improvement comes through trial and error. My mistakes were sprinkled with a few successes; but always I felt growth and great contentment from the fellowship of sharing the experiences with other quilters. I would continuously strive to improve my technical skills.

As my interest in smaller scale grew, there were very few patterns available in sizes I wanted to work with, so I decided to draft my own. I made a lot of mistakes, but my excitement and confidence grew with each project.

Errors highlight opportunities for learning, but with practice, it gets easier to identify mistakes and develop solutions. Finding those solutions is how we develop our creativity and also where we can have the most fun.

For those in the process of discovery, growth, and continuous improvement, *The Art of Machine Piecing* is a how-to reference that offers detailed information regarding drafting, achieving precision workmanship, and choosing fabric and color relative to smaller scale work. My wish is that this book helps you find the joy that awaits each of us in the journey of the technical process. Enjoy your journey!

1 *Philosophy and Creativity*

In contrast to the world of fast-quick-easy-painless-fearless and magical, I am suggesting an approach to quiltmaking that rests upon the value of spending the time necessary to achieve quality work. Enjoy the journey from idea to reality. Appreciate the challenge of executing precise technique, experience the satisfaction of doing your best, and to honor the work that gives a heartbeat to creative ideas. These are a few of the advantages and benefits of this approach.

After the design lines and shapes have been determined and blended with our color and fabric choices, a vision begins its journey from our mind's eye to its physical reality. As each part of the quiltmaking process (color, design, drafting, cutting, sewing, pinning, pressing, finishing) is executed with skill and care, beautiful quilts emerge. Quality workmanship and piecing detail make the defining difference between ordinary quilts and extraordinary ones. The truism, anything worth doing is worth doing well, clearly expresses the nobility of thoughtful work. This book combines my love of sewing and small scale piecing with an ongoing affection for making 3" square traditional style patchwork blocks. I have very consciously and concisely examined all the details that have sharpened and improved my sewing and creative skills and share them with you. I quite simply emptied my head of all the information, ideas, philosophy and techniques I know to accomplish quality work. I use forty-nine sampler blocks as tools to illustrate and explain this information. Each block offers its own gifts of fun, challenge and growth as you learn to examine, critique, and correct your own work. Discovering how stimulating and enlightening problem solving can be is the purpose of this journey.

As is often the case, a small change or a tiny detail can make large differences in a final product, so please take the time to read through the entire book before beginning to sew. Although this book includes the complete pattern and instructions for the featured quilt, *My Journey*, and several project ideas, I encourage you to use the individual blocks to your own best advantage. Discover the gifts each block has to offer. Combine them in your own way, create your own designs, and broaden your experience.

Spend the time you need to take pleasure in the journey, where joy and rewards await your discoveries.

Philosophy

The single largest influence on our ability to succeed is attitude. The basic truth is: if we think we can, we will; if we think we can't, we won't. Attitude is the first choice we make, and it is one we have exclusive control over. Choosing a positive attitude ensures eventual success of any goal. The goal of quality workmanship is attainable for everybody and anybody who chooses it and is willing to work for it.

When we make the choice for improving skills, we begin a satisfying journey to quality. Being open to making mistakes, open to learning new ideas, techniques, and methods, and open to practicing those experiences is a path to freedom. You become aware of what's wrong and discover how to correct your errors and continue moving forward.

Errors or mistakes are temporary departures from accuracy. We should view them as gifts, or as private tutoring. They point out opportunities for success. I believe many people see their errors as failures because they don't know how or why it happened, or what is required to correct the error. If we shift our attitude about mistakes from failure to opportunity to succeed, we open ourselves to the intended experiences of learning. We grow, improve, and raise our awareness.

Mistakes are important necessary steps in learning. Discovering how and why errors happen, and understanding how to convert them into success is the valuable bi-product of experience.

Mistakes nurture our creative problem-solving skills, and problem solving is a real key to finding the joy in quiltmaking. We want to quickly recognize and honor our mistakes, understand how they happened, correct them, and carry that experience forward. Learning to critique and correct our own work builds both self-confidence and beautiful quilts. The only time a mistake is a problem is when we make the same mistake again and again.

Quality workmanship does not mean we sew perfectly every time. It does mean we know how to get out of trouble. Perfection is not the goal for me; continuous improvement is the prize. Little fairies do not drop from the heavens and determine whose work will be great and whose will not! We are responsible for our own work.

In my experience, achieving quality requires four basic things:

1. Choosing a positive attitude, open and willing to make mistakes.
2. Learning to identify mistakes through evaluation and critique.
3. Learning why the mistake happened and how to correct it.
4. A willingness to do the work (practice) required to achieve quality work.

Achieving a high level of quality depends on how we execute each individual step in the process: how well we choose design, color and fabric; how accurately we draft, cut and sew; how well we trim or grade seams, pin, press, measure, make corrections, baste, quilt and bind contribute to the ultimate quality of our completed quilt. Each step, done with skill and care and in concert with each other, results in quality. Each is equally important to the whole, and no single step is any more or less important than any other step.

If you struggle with a specific technique, or part of the block doesn't measure what it should, or points are incomplete, or an intersection does not match, it's at these steps you make a choice for quality. Examine the problem, determine what's wrong, and decide what's needed to correct it; or choose to be frustrated, blame your machine (or whatever else is handy) and stop your journey. It is at these times we learn the most. When I experience the toughest challenges, I know it means I need to improve my performance in one or more steps in the process.

I also know that quality work does not just happen at the end by "squaring up" my block. It starts at the beginning as each part interrelates with the next. Quality is a cumulative process, not a singular achievement.

If you truly want to improve your sewing skills and add to your quiltmaking experience, you start with a change of attitude. It is a minor but profound shift. "I could never do that" becomes "I want to improve, show me how." I have often heard students say things like: "If you can't notice the mistake when riding by on a galloping horse it's acceptable." Quality is between you and your quilt, as you define "quality," but it should not be dependent upon time constraints or standards that are too forgiving.

When I knowingly leave an error in one of my quilts, I can't help but point it out whenever I show the quilt. We cannot fool ourselves, and we're not fooling anyone else, so what's the point to ignoring those opportunities. I can tell you from my own experience, when people view quilts on display, whether or not they quilt, are men or women, younger or older, they forget about how much time it took to make the quilt, but they always remember how well it was done.

We demand and expect only the best quality fabrics for our quilts. We want only the highest quality sewing machines and tools. Are not our quilts just as worthy of a similar choice for quality workmanship?

I encourage every quilter to thoughtfully honor the workmanship that brings ideas to life. Giving your quilts your personal best is giving yourself a rare gift. You and they deserve it. Remember to enjoy the journey; it is all we really have.

Creativity

I can't think of any word or concept that I was more uncomfortable about than creative or creativity. I remember my teachers talking about being creative, and I had no clue about what it meant to create. When I first began making quilts, I would see quilts at shows, in books, or in magazines, and I would buy patterns and make them. I wanted them to be exactly what I saw. I began by imitating and emulating the work of others. I loved that, and believe there is nothing wrong with that.

With time, I began to experience the joy and bliss that quiltmaking gives each of us. I slowly began to design my own work, develop my own style, and discover, or awaken my own creativity. I have learned that I do not actually "create anything" new, but rather I take inspiration from the things I see around me, from events that happen to me, or often from serendipity.

The inspiration can come from a photo, a pleasing color scheme, a favorite fabric, a newly discovered block, or a time-honored traditional block. The creative process is one of pulling various existing parts into a new or different whole. It is not originating, or creating the parts and the whole, as much as it is noticing and orchestrating the beauty that is already all around us. Understanding this was an unburdening kind of discovery, a release from a scary unknown that I can now sometimes laugh about, even if I still do not fully understand it.

I turned from imitation to imagination when I realized the biggest obstacle in my way was my own confidence, and I gave myself permission to make mistakes, lots of them, and to learn from them. I began to see mistakes as positive tools that would only help me grow. I honor them as opportunities and gifts, and I take full advantage of them.

We are all creative. I believe creativity grows, emerges and blossoms when you have a real love for what you are doing.

It appears to me that our creative self most probably emerges in those activities we are involved in with love. It is a kind of energy that carries us to and from love, and it is strengthened by use. I recommend keeping a "want-to-do" list. Haven't you found yourself thinking, or saying aloud: "I've always wanted to do a swag border, or I want to work in purple and orange," or "What happens if I turn this block on point," or "I want to try a Medallion style quilt." Keeping track of these "want to's" will remind you to add or incorporate one or more of them into your next project.

Look at quilts in books and magazines or at quilt shows and notice what you like or do not like. Note the color scheme, the borders, quilting designs, set, shapes, and sizes. Use what appeals to you in your next quilt. Find specific elements you like from different quilts and combine them in your own way. Become aware of discovering, acknowledging, and understanding what you do not like, as much as what you do like, as this is equally important information.

Confidence seems to grow from knowing our own preferences. Also, your level of awareness grows or broadens the more you examine the world around you in terms of how each part should be incorporated or left out of your work. The next time you find yourself remaking someone else's quilt, change something. Just one change is a beginning step toward awakening your own creativity, and hopefully you will find that same unburdening that I discovered.

II Tools and Equipment

In addition to the usual quiltmaking tools, I also use the following to help me achieve quality workmanship.

1/16" HOLE PUNCH

An invaluable tool for template making. (See Source list, page 125.)

ADHESIVE SANDPAPER DOTS, SMALL

I place these dots on appropriate corners of my rulers to help them grab the mat and/or fabric and prevent slipping when cutting.

BIAS OR CELTIC BARS™ (METAL)

I prefer metal to other materials because metal forms a flat, well-creased bias piece.

COMPASS

I use a compass to draft a simple eight-pointed star.

CUTTING MAT, SMALL

Used when subcutting or custom cutting small pieces or units, because it is easier to manage and keeps work more accurate to rotate the mat than to move and disturb the fabric. I always cut on the ungridded side of the mat, as grids are not always accurate for measuring and cutting.

FLANNEL DESIGN BOARD

30" × 40" or 11$\frac{1}{2}$" × 13$\frac{1}{2}$" foam-core board, covered with flannel, to use for designing. You can pin into it and take it to your machine. These are simply smaller versions of a design wall. The 11$\frac{1}{2}$" × 13$\frac{1}{2}$" size fits into the two-gallon size zippered bags.

HOT TAPE™

Holds appliqué shapes in place instead of thread basting or pinning. You can iron on it, remove it with no residue, and reuse it. Hot Tape can be bought in general fabric stores.

INSTANT CAMERA OR DIGITAL CAMERA

Quickly photograph work in progress, change it around to get different looks, evaluate value placement and other potential problems and be able to move the work back to its original position without having to sketch or remember.

MIRRORS

Two (3$\frac{1}{2}$" × 6" approx.) mirrors taped together at one end to see how borders will turn the corner, to reproduce one image multiple times, and numerous other design uses.

MULTIFACETED VIEWER

An inexpensive tool (found in toy shops) to view multiples of one block, to place those blocks on square or on point, and to see how the color is working.

PINS

I usc IBC Super Fine Silk Pins #5004 (1$\frac{1}{4}$" × .50mm). They feel finer and create less disturbance when sewing.

QUILTERS' GLUTUBE®

Allows me to create very small appliqué shapes successfully and easily. Do not confuse this with a glue stick.

REDUCING GLASS

Gives distance from the work, which allows evaluation of fabric, color, and value choices.

ROTARY CUTTER, SMALL

Easy to hold and control.

ROUND WOODEN TOOTHPICK

I find this an invaluable tool to scoot fabric under when appliquéing. The wood gently grasps the cotton fabric and makes it very easy to manipulate small seam allowances. It is also helpful if a knot reappears and you need to separate the cotton fibers to push it back into the quilt.

ROXANNE'S GLUE-BASTE-IT™

Watersoluble glue with a fine needle-nose applicator.

RULERS

I use a 3" × 18" Omnigrid® ruler with a continuous $^1/_8$" grid marked with very fine black lines both horizontally and vertically. I also use a 4" square Omnigrid ruler with the above-mentioned black line $^1/_8$" grid. These rulers are accurate and easy to read because, even though I sew with $^1/_4$" seam allowances, I often cut in $^1/_8$" increments.

SANDPAPER BOARD

Can be made from a 12" or 13" square of Masonite™ with a sheet of very fine sandpaper glued to it. I use this to place fabric on when tracing around templates because it gently grabs the fabric and prevents it from moving.

SERRATED-EDGE SCISSORS, 4" AND 8"

These are very helpful to maintain an exact straight line when trimming seams and cutting out template shapes from fabric, because the serration prevents the fabric from slipping off the edge.

SEWING MACHINE

I use a Pfaff® 7550.

SEWING MACHINE NEEDLE

I use Schmetz Microtex 60/8 or 70/10.

SEWING THREAD

DMC® 50 weight, 2 ply Machine Embroidery thread, 100% mercerized cotton. I use this for machine piecing and machine quilting. Fine, strong, takes up less space.

STILETTO

A pointed tool used when machine sewing as an extension of your hand.

STRAIGHT STITCH THROAT PLATE

Essential for machine piecing and quilting for nice straight stitching. It also prevents your machine from "eating" small pieces because the small hole is less opportunity for fabric to enter than the usual zigzag throat plate.

TWEEZERS

Helpful in removing small paper shapes from appliqué work.

ZIPPERED BAGS

I use various sizes for storing templates, completed blocks, blocks in progress, small design foam-core boards or whole quilts so they can be kept clean and can be seen and shared without handling.

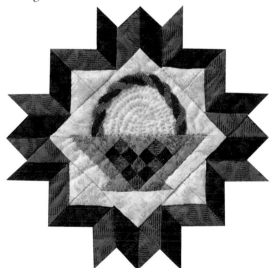

III Color and Fabric

After writing my book *Small Scale Quiltmaking* I continued my efforts to understand color and its many influences. I have taken classes, read as much as I can, and practiced as many approaches as I could think of; and after a pretty fair effort, I can happily but humbly say that color and I have become a bit more friendly. I offer this experience to all who have found the path to being comfortable with color decisions as challenging as I found it.

Getting good at choosing color and fabric does not happen overnight. You gain and accumulate experience with each quilt and carry that experience forward with each project. Successful color choices and a deeper understanding of color are parts of an ongoing journey. This is a process that seems to improve with time, practice, patience, experimentation, and study. Knowing how colors relate to each other to create harmony and balance in your quilt will happen as you become more at ease and familiar with color. Working with colors you love, treating the process as an ongoing string of decisions (no single decision ends the process, it just leads you to the next choice), and being persistent about not letting the choosing end until your heart is genuinely happy are what produce the most satisfying results for me.

Color is what most of us see first. It grabs our attention as we view quilts. We react to color emotionally, (positively, negatively or indifferently). We respond to color more than any other element of a quilt. The challenge is to create a quilt that is balanced in both color and design, which embraces the viewer from a distance and draws them closer.

As you go to quilt shows, or look at quilt magazines and books, deliberately notice only color and take physical or mental notes on what you like, what color combinations are you drawn to, do you like muted or pure colors, pastels, etc. Make notes as well of what you do not like. Determine if you prefer one-color or two-color quilts; maybe scrap quilts are your favorite.

Become aware of the quilts that make you "ooh and ah." Think about why they cause you to react the way you do. Are traditional style quilts your favorite, or is it the art quilts that appeal most strongly to you. Through this process you can begin to know your own preferences, and that understanding helps to develop your own quiltmaking style.

The quilts I often "ooh and ah" about are those that seem to have a tapestrylike color and design feeling. These quilts integrate the blocks or design area with the background so that they become one rather than separate entities. I discovered the difference between those quilts and the quilts I was making was the choice of color in the background area versus my typical white-on-white or beige-on-beige background fabrics.

As I began a quilt or block, I would choose my colors; let's say red, blue, and gold. Then I would get a so-called "background" fabric, which usually had no color or visual texture and was rather uninteresting. I began to understand that using one of the chosen colors in the background area helped to integrate the design and background. This concept is well demonstrated in the more recent blocks of the featured quilt, *My Journey*, page 104, and shows in the *Small Scale Medallion Sampler*, *Diamond Jubilee*, and *Circle of Stars* quilts. The look is pleasing, and is achieved by simply making the background area one of your chosen colors and manipulating the values to create the desired block or quilt design.

A comment I commonly receive about these recent quilts is "they look like a tapestry."

Noticing what you like, and determining how you can achieve that look, is challenging, exciting, humbling, and most of all, fun!

Some ways to nudge your color sense or decide a color scheme in your quilts or blocks might be:

- Develop a "color inspiration" file. Look through magazines, quilt-related or not, and when you see a quilt that you love because of its color, tear it out and place it in the file. Maybe it's a catalog or home decor magazine. If you see a beautiful room or table setting or linen ad or whatever in colors that please you, tear it out and place it in your file. It doesn't have to be a quilt to be a beautiful color palette. It will, at the very least, serve as a stepping stone.
- A fabric with beautiful colors, regardless of print or content, works the same way as a page from a magazine. Use the color as inspiration even if you never use the actual fabric in your quilts. The fabric will have served its purpose.
- You could choose color for a quilt by knowing its purpose, or reason for making it, if it has one. For example, is it a holiday quilt (Christmas/red and green, Easter/pastels, Autumn/earth tones, oranges, browns, etc.)? Maybe it's a gift for a friend and you would use their favorite color(s).
- Maybe you want an Amish style quilt, an old-fashioned style, a Victorian style, or a contemporary style. These styles would lead you to obvious color choices.

- Nature always suggests a beautiful variety of palettes like seascapes, seasons, flowers, and foliage. Inspiration for color is all around us. Begin to look with color in mind. Once you have an inspirational image or object, use it to pick your colors and fabrics. Look at the fabric or image and identify each color you see in it. Examine it carefully and do not miss any of the subtleties. Pull fabrics from your shelf (or the quilt shop shelves) that have those colors. Keep proportion in mind. If the inspiration fabric, image,

Diamond Jubilee

Circle of Stars

Medallion Sampler

Palette fabric

Color Wheel

Red
Red-orange
Orange
Yellow-orange
Yellow
Yellow-green
Green
Blue-green
Blue
Blue-violet
Purple (violet)
Red-violet

Gizmo

or object is mostly pinks, with few greens, and a touch of gold, choose the fabric proportionately. Make your group of fabrics look like the inspiration piece and maintain the color integrity and proportion.

♦ Expand or stretch each color to its greatest potential. Develop a range of values from light to dark within the intensity that is apparent in your inspiration. Vary the visual texture, or size and style of the print on the fabric to develop a good mix. Include a bright and a deep dark. You do not have to use each one, just develop a full palette with lots of choices.

I encourage you to become familiar with and develop a basic understanding of the color wheel. The most basic level of understanding of the wheel is still a very valuable asset. It has helped me realize that even though I rarely use the exact colors on the color wheel, they are the source from which all my choices evolve. I understand simple things like colors opposite one another on the color wheel are complements, and they make each other look great. Two or three colors next to one another on the color wheel (analogous) work together and an accent color is across the wheel. Start somewhere, read the books recommended in the bibliography, page 125, and take the first steps.

My own understanding of the color wheel is quite basic, but it helps me quickly find solutions.

Value

Value is the amount of lightness or darkness in a color. Adding black to pure colors creates shades (dark values). Adding white to pure colors creates tints (light values). Adding gray to pure colors creates tones (medium values). Shades, tints and tones of color are all values ranging from light to dark. Value is also relative and relies on the surrounding values to define itself. For example, a light value fabric will become medium when surrounded by or placed next to a fabric of lighter value. Value placement is also what creates design although color gets most of the applause.

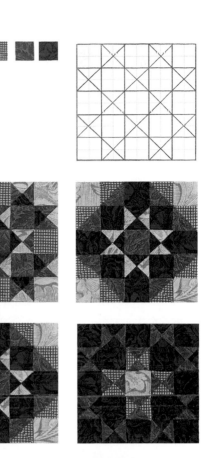

Light   *Medium*   *Dark*

Relative value

Value Contrast

Value contrast is the degree of difference between touching values. You can develop high exaggerated contrast or low subtle contrast. Small piecing especially benefits from high, exaggerated value contrast, which allows the viewer to clearly read the design from a distance.

The intensity or saturation of color is how pure and brilliant or how grayed and dull it is.

Value placement creates design

High contrast   *Subtle contrast*

Noteworthy

The smaller you cut color the darker it will get.

Visual Texture

Visual texture of fabric is the size and style of the print on the fabric. Successful quilts in any size require a variety of visual textures to create interest. There is an enormous amount of options and choices in visual texture for quilters today; be sure your shelf includes them all.

Collect large, medium, and small floral and foliage type fabrics, plaids, stripes, and checks printed regularly or irregularly.

Also include ethnic and theme prints (stars, dogs, vegetables, fruit, etc.), dots, circles, and bubbles. Have on hand feathers, paisleys, pebbles, grass, sky, as well as abstract and true geometric patterns. You are not required to love every print you buy. I find it helpful, when working small especially, to cut out shapes from 3" × 5" cards in the sizes I use most often and use them to help me read or know how fabrics will cut up by placing it on bolts of fabric when I shop. Using a variety of visual texture in your quilts or blocks is what adds interest and detail to your quilts. Just remember to create balance, not chaos.

Tone-on-tone fabrics are usually two or more values of

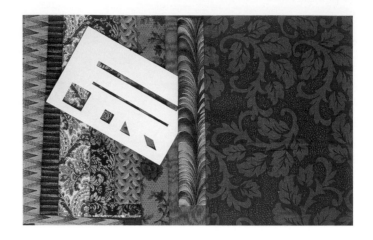

one color with subtle but effective visual texture. They can read as solids from a distance, have low activity and add quietness without distraction. I use this type of fabric often in small shapes to enhance and support more active, larger scaled, multi-colored prints in larger shapes. If you have a starring role fabric, you must surround it with supporting role fabrics to make it stand out.

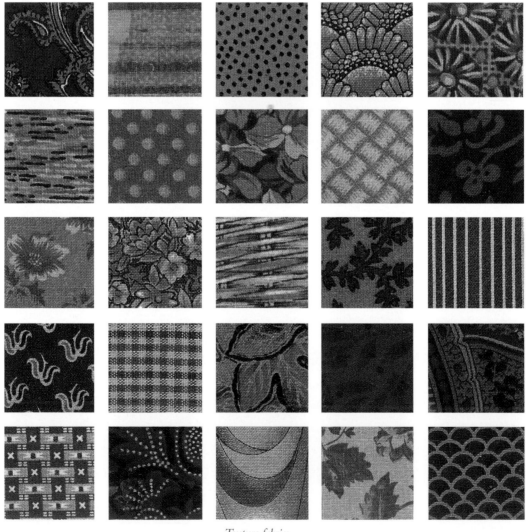

Texture fabrics

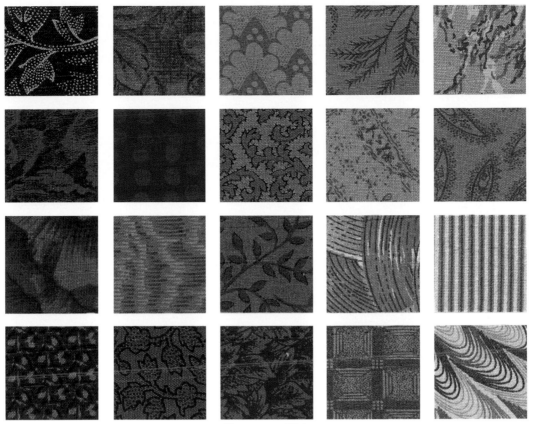

Tone-on-tone fabrics

Border prints add elegance, sophistication, and detail to quilts. Most quilters look at the wider areas of border prints, but I often use the more narrow areas in small work and in blocks. In addition to the obvious use as borders, this type of print can be custom cut using templates, and used in other ways as well. In particular, the pieced border in the featured quilt, *My Journey*, page 104, takes advantage of a border print by custom cutting a triangle shape from the same place. Blocks using borders prints are Interlocking Squares, page 66, Jack-in-the-Box, page 65, Charleston Quilt, page 103, and Hens and Chickens Variation, page 74.

I continue to avoid fabrics that have random areas of white in them as they can be distracting and fall at the tip of a triangle and if using a light background, can make good sewing look bad.

I try to take advantage of or exploit fabric to the utmost. Visual print used creatively, especially in small piecing, adds interest, unexpected detail, and integrity to all quilts.

Helpful Strategies

As I compose blocks or quilts, there are a few things I think about and evaluate when my work just isn't the way I think it should be. Try incorporating one or more of the following ideas, and see if they might help your work too. I do know, from experience, that often the smallest change can make the biggest difference.

♦ If you find your eye travels all over your quilt, try adding a very dark value of one color in small amounts to give the work order, unity, and a resting place for the eye.

♦ If your block or quilt seems dull or flat and uninteresting, add a bright (high intensity) of one of the colors, again in small amounts. A little goes a long way.

♦ Evaluate and determine if your block or quilt seems too busy and chaotic. You might need to quiet your block or quilt by replacing some of the busy printed fabrics with low activity, quiet fabrics. Remember, if you have a great fabric to "star" in your quilt, you will need to surround it with quiet, supporting-role fabrics to be able to appreciate the "star."

- View your work through a reducing glass and if anything really pops out, that is usually the area that needs changing. Maybe the color is right but the value or intensity needs improvement.
- Perhaps the contrast is too exaggerated or too subtle.
- Perhaps the proportion of your colors needs improvement. Equal amounts of all your colors can create confusion. I usually have one dominant color, then a secondary important color, and then an accent color used in small amounts. Good proportion of each color will help to create balance and order. Usually blocks have mostly background color, then design area color, and then an accent color is added in smaller areas. Proportion in size and scale of prints is also a consideration.
- Don't expect to make all the right choices initially, just get something on your design area and then you have something to change and refine.
- One, two, or three colors in a variety of values and intensities can often be more successful than lots of different colors. Some of the most beautiful, spectacular quilts are monochromatic. Keeping it simple is always a good choice.

Blocks are a great way to practice color principles. Use blocks for this purpose even if you only do mock-ups and no sewing. They will become valuable reference material.

Fabric

Fabric Preparation

I only recommend using high quality 100 percent cotton fabric. Cotton is dependable, soft, manageable, easy to finger crease, substantial in weight when sewing, presses well, and is an absolute must for small piecework. Having said that, know that cotton fabric is fluid and moves as you cut, sew, press and quilt. Be aware of that, and forgive yourself as you make your blocks, quilts, and garments.

My preference is to prewash my fabrics. I do not do anything special. I wash my fabrics as I wash my clothes, and I put them in the dryer. From the dryer, I fold and place the fabric in my storage shelving, and press only when I'm ready to cut and construct blocks.

I usually purchase quarter or third yard pieces of fabric. If I need fabric for borders, I buy enough fabric to use the lengthwise grain because it eliminates stretching and insures successful straight borders. When I find a fabric I can't live without, I buy three yards.

Fabric Grain

Grain in fabric is the lengthwise (warp) and crosswise (weft) threads that are woven together to create the cloth. Crosswise grain runs from selvage to selvage and has some stretch depending upon the thread count and the weave. Lengthwise grain runs parallel to the selvage and has very little, if any, stretch. Both cross and lengthwise grains are described as straight grain. Placing the straight of the grain on the outside edges of your blocks or quilt is most important to maintain accurate measurements and keeping your work square.

Noteworthy
To please the eye, directional fabrics should be cut with the print or pattern of the fabric rather than the grain if a discrepancy exists between the two.

Random bias is anything other than cross or lengthwise grain and has some stretch. True bias runs on a 45° angle to the cross and lengthwise grain and has the maximum amount of stretch.

When using templates, grain arrows should be aligned with the straight of grain. Bias edges will stretch, can create ripples and waves, and be difficult to control. However, I never sacrifice fabric design for grain. If I want a particular motif or part of a fabric to be positioned in a certain way that results in exposed bias edges, I just handle and sew it very carefully. I am extremely respectful of bias and keep the iron away from exposed bias edges whenever possible.

Successful quiltmaking in any size requires careful attention to grain placement and the blocks, projects and techniques described in this book will be specific about grain.

IV Design

Drafting

I am always thankful that my entrance into the quilt community was at a time when drafting, making templates, and scissor cutting fabric, were the most commonly applied techniques.

Drafting has enabled me to better understand the workings of the design. Clearly seeing how the design fits together, and in what order the pieces are to be sewn, has helped develop my confidence to be more creative and original while drafting. Those basic original skills have a synergistic value to them that fosters a freedom to explore, and drafting develops a healthy respect for the importance of accuracy when sewing.

The following overview offers some basic insight into drafting. It is a small, simplistic peek into a huge world, and I sincerely urge you to advance your study of drafting by referring to the publications listed in the bibliography and doing your own experimenting. You will love this journey.

The tools needed for drafting are few but important.

- ♦ Accurate graph paper, eight squares to the inch, seven squares to the inch, and ten squares to the inch, with darkened one-inch lines. (See Sources—page 125).
- ♦ A No. 2 mechanical pencil (the disposable ones work fine).
- ♦ A good eraser—do not rely on the end of the pencil.
- ♦ Accurate ruler—2" × 12" or 2" × 18" C-Thru® Ruler with red lines and eight-to-the-inch grid divisions, or see the 3" × 18" ruler described in Tools and Equipment—page 8. Shop at art supply or drafting stores for this purchase.

- ♦ A good compass. Cheap ones do not hold their position.
- ♦ Six-inch square ruler, or a drafting triangle.

Most patchwork designs fit into or are developed on a grid. A grid is the number of squares (in this case) a block pattern is divided into, much like a checkerboard. Shapes such as triangles, rectangles, parallelograms, etc., are developed or superimposed over the grid by connecting or eliminating lines to create the design.

There are four basic grid drafting categories that much of patchwork fits into. Four-patch, five-patch, seven-patch, and nine-patch drafting category means or indicates that the block is divided into exactly that number of total divisions or multiples of that number.

Successful pattern drafting first requires that you look at a block design or pattern and visually divide it into equal units or sections or grids. The easiest way to determine what drafting category a block pattern falls into is to identify the number of equal divisions across the top or down the side of the block, or along one long seam; or go to the smallest piece and count.

If you count two, four, or eight equal divisions, along one edge, your block would be a four-patch, and the number of equal divisions would give you the appropriate grid formation to then develop your block pattern.

Noteworthy

When you do not have the suggested graph paper refer to page 21, Draft Any Size Square Into Any Size Grid.

Four-Patch

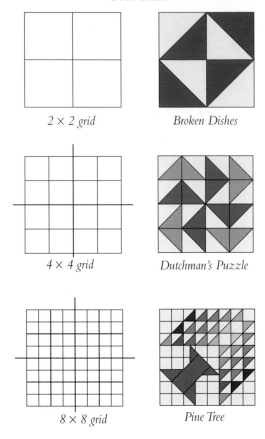

2 × 2 grid

Broken Dishes

4 × 4 grid

Dutchman's Puzzle

8 × 8 grid

Pine Tree

If you count three or six or nine equal divisions, your block would be a nine-patch drafting category and the number of equal divisions would give you the appropriate grid formation to develop your block pattern.

Nine-Patch

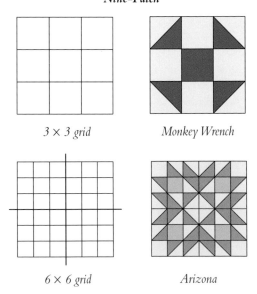

3 × 3 grid

Monkey Wrench

6 × 6 grid

Arizona

If you count five or ten equal divisions, your block would be a five-patch, and the number of equal divisions would give you the appropriate grid formation to develop your block pattern.

Five-Patch

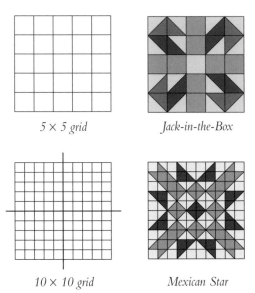

5 × 5 grid

Jack-in-the-Box

10 × 10 grid

Mexican Star

If you count seven or fourteen equal divisions, your block would be a seven-patch, and the number of equal divisions would give you the appropriate grid formation to develop the block pattern.

Seven-Patch

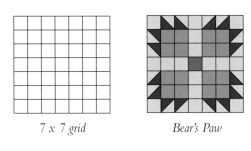

7 x 7 grid

Bear's Paw

Another very common drafting category is the eight-pointed star. This design or block is developed from radiating lines out from the center of a square rather than an equal grid of squares. There are other drafting categories that are not discussed here such as five pointed star designs, hexagons, and more advanced eight-pointed star designs. I encourage you to refer to the recommended reading material, page 125, for further valuable study. The information here is simply a stepping stone. Begin the drafting process and own your own work.

Begin Your Drafting Journey

1. Choose a block design you want to make. For this exercise we will choose a Friendship Star. Keep in mind your preference for cutting: rotary cutting or templates. Your sewing skill will determine the type of pattern to some extent. The more complicated the block (this often has to do with how many pieces are in the block), the more sewing skill is required.

2. Determine the drafting category or basic grid of your chosen block design. (Is it a nine-patch, four-patch, five-patch, seven-patch, or eight-pointed star?) The Friendship Star is a nine-patch drafting category with a 3 × 3 grid.

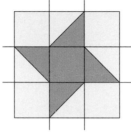

3. Decide on the size of the block you want to make (we will draft a 6" block). Although blocks can be drafted in any size you desire, it is easiest to choose a size of block that is easily divisible by the number of grids across or down the pattern. For example, if your block is a four-patch drafting category with a sixteen-square grid (4 × 4), it would be easily drafted into a 4", 6", 8", 10", or 12" block size, because those sizes are all divisible by four. Similarly, if your chosen block is a nine-patch drafting category with a 36-square grid (6 × 6), it would be easily drafted into 3", 4$\frac{1}{2}$", 6", 7$\frac{1}{2}$", etc. All are easily divisible by six.

4. Draw the chosen size of square on graph paper. For this exercise, draw a 6" square on eight squares-to-the-inch graph paper. You would use ten squares-to-the-inch graph paper for five-patch drafting category blocks and whenever numbers work out in tenths.

Noteworthy

There is often confusion about what finished and unfinished means when block sizes are stated in books and patterns. To clarify, finished indicates the block size without any seam allowances included, i.e., 3" finished block. Unfinished indicates the block size including a $\frac{1}{4}$" seam allowance on all sides, i.e., 3$\frac{1}{2}$" unfinished block. Drafting and designing do not include any seam allowances. Seam allowances are added only when it is time to cut and sew.

Tip: Using a pencil and ruler to make lines exactly on graph paper lines, to connect corners and dots exactly, or to make perfect diagonal lines, you must position your ruler's edge away from the specific area slightly to allow for the width of the pencil. To see clearly and avoid creating shadows when drafting, position your light source on the side of your ruler with the pencil.

5. Determine the basic grid dimension and draw the grid within the 6" square. The grid dimension is the measurement or size of each division of the square. For example, for our exercise we are drafting a 6" Friendship Star that is a nine-patch drafting category (3 × 3). To determine the grid dimension, divide the size of the block (6") by the number of equal divisions (3), i.e., 6" ÷ by 3 divisions = 2" grid dimension.

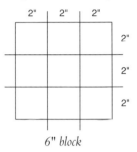

6" block

Noteworthy

You can easily change the size of your block by changing the grid dimension. For example, if your grid was 1" you would have a 3" block. If the grid was $\frac{1}{2}$" you would have a 1$\frac{1}{2}$" block, if the grid dimension was 3" you would have a 9" block. The grid dimension determines the size of the block.

6. Referring to your photo, line drawing, or image, develop the block design by subdividing the grid. As you continue to draft your own patterns, you will find that in some designs not all grid lines will become seam lines.

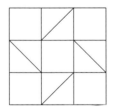

7. Identify the shapes needed to sew the block and put in the grain lines, keeping straight grain on the outside edges of the block. In the Friendship Star there are only two shapes, a right angle triangle Shape A and a square Shape B.

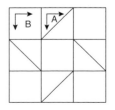

8. Examine the design and determine the logical sewing sequence to piece the block. One way to do this is to first find the longest lines, usually but not always, they will run from edge to edge horizontally, vertically, or diagonally. Blocks are usually assembled by first joining pieces into units, then units into rows, then rows into the completed block.

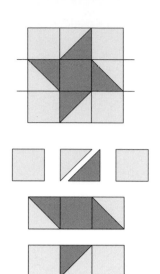

9. To be able to sew the design, you now need to determine the cutting dimensions by isolating the shapes, adding $1/4"$ seam allowance on all sides, and then measuring the shape. When measuring the shape for cutting, if the dimensions are easily found on the ruler then rotary cutting would be the method of cutting. If the size is not easily found on the ruler (for me this is anything beyond $1/8"$ increments), I make a template (page 27) for that shape. For example, the A triangle is a 2" half-square triangle finished (2" on the short sides). If you want to be able to cut a square in half that will yield two triangle shapes that include $1/4"$ seam allowance on all three sides, simply measure that triangle shape from corner to tip, after you have added the seam allowance, cut your square that size, then cut again diagonally.

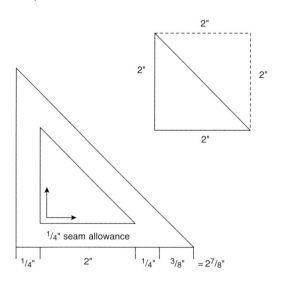

The same is true for cutting a quarter-square triangle. If you isolate and measure the long leg of the quarter-square triangle in a 6" Ohio Star block, for example, it measures 2". Add $1/4"$ seam allowance on all three sides, and you will be able to cut a square the finished size plus $1 1/4"$, or in this case, $3 1/4"$ square, and cut this square into quarters diagonally. Again, no magic. The measurement exists if you measure from tip to tip, you are adding an additional $6/8"$ ($3/8"$ on each tip) to the usual $1/2"$ seam allowance ($1/4"$ on each tip).

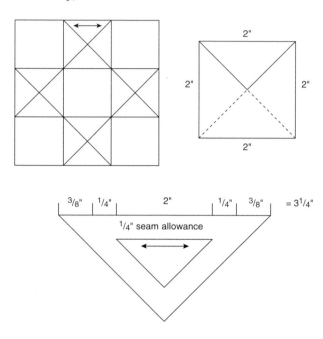

That is where those so called magic numbers come from, no mystery, they are there and exist. You will always add $7/8"$ to the finished short side of a half-square triangle to get the size of the square you need to be able to cut two triangles from it that include $1/4"$ seam allowance on all three sides. Similarly, you will always add $1 1/4"$ to the finished long side of a quarter-square triangle to know the size of the square you need to be able to cut four triangles from it that include $1/4"$ seam allowance on all three sides.

Draft Any Size Square Into Any Size Grid

There are times that you will want to draft a block that does not fit easily into the size of the square you want. For example, if you want to draft a 6" Bear's Paw block, which is a seven-patch drafting category (7 × 7 grid), you need to divide a 6" square into seven equal divisions across and down or forty-nine total. To do this:

1. Draw the size square you desire on any graph or plain paper (in this case a 6" square), and identify the four corners 1, 2, 3, 4.

2. Find a measurement on your ruler that is larger than the block size and that is also divisible by seven (the number of equal division across and down). That would be the 7" mark on your ruler. Seven is divisible by seven and is larger than the 6" block you chose (7 ÷ 7 = 1").

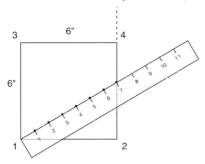

3. Position one end of your ruler on the left corner 1 of your 6" square. Angle the ruler up until the 7" mark on the ruler is on the right edge line of the square.

4. Make a dot on your paper every 1" (this is the number you arrived at by dividing seven into seven in Step 2. Mark exactly, not casually.

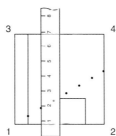

5. Position a square ruler on the bottom edge of your paper as well as on the first dot. This creates an accurate 90° angle. Place your longer ruler next to the square, remove the square and draw a vertical line going right through the dot. Repeat for all the dots across the square.

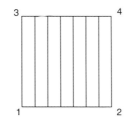

6. Turn your paper one quarter turn and repeat Steps 3, 4, 5 to create the 7 × 7 grid in the 6" square needed to then draft the Bear's Paw block or any 6" seven-patch block.

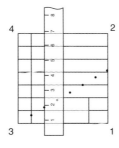

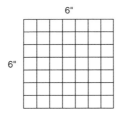

Noteworthy
Referring to Step 2, if the number you need doesn't fit on the square, extend the right edge line upward to accommodate the ruler in order to reach the desired number.

Draft a Simple Eight-Pointed Star

1. Draw a square of any desired size on graph or plain paper.

2. Draw light lines horizontally, vertically, and diagonally on the square. This identifies the center and gives needed reference lines for drafting.

3. Place the point of your compass at the center and open the compass so that the pencil is at one of the corners. Hold this position on the compass. Now move the point of the compass to the left corner and swivel the pencil so it lightly marks the two lines that extend from that corner.

4. Repeat for the remaining three corners.

5. Label these markings A and B as shown. Connect each A to two B's. Erase appropriate lines to clarify the three template shapes needed for a simple eight-pointed LeMoyne Star block—a square, a triangle and a true 45° diamond.

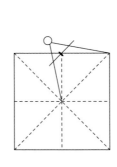

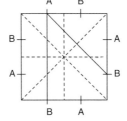

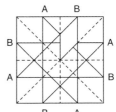

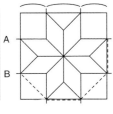

Notice that the equality present in this category is not the distance between the three divisions along the edge of the block but the distance from one star point to another.

Measure and Monitor Patchwork

As discussed in the drafting section, most square patchwork blocks are developed on a grid of equal divisions across and down the square. Grid dimension refers to the size of each individual square and determines the size of the block, it does not include seam allowance. To be able to measure your work as you sew, you must first know what the grid dimension is.

You can determine this information in two different ways:

1. Decide the block pattern you want to design (Friendship Star), identify the drafting category (nine-patch, 3 × 3 grid) and choose a block size (3"). Then, to find out the grid dimension, simply **divide** the size of the block by the number of equal divisions across the edge of the design. For example: 3" (block size) divided by 3 (number of equal division across the block) equals 1" grid dimension.

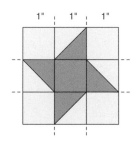

2. Another way to determine or know the grid dimension of a block is to choose one. For example, let's say you want to do a Friendship Star block (nine-patch, 3 × 3 grid) and you are comfortable sewing in a $1/2$" finished grid. The block size is determined by **multiplying** the grid dimension ($1/2$") by the number of equal divisions across the block (3): $1/2$" × 3 equals $1 1/2$" block size. I do this if I'm only making one block or if I'm doing a repeat block quilt because the size of the block is not as important as working in a grid dimension I'm comfortable with. I also reduce the grid dimension when I want to challenge myself and practice sewing in a smaller grid dimension.

If the grid dimension plus seam allowance is not a number easily found on my ruler (the smallest fraction I use with rulers is eighths) and I'm using templates to cut with, I use the template to evaluate and monitor the patchwork by placing each template on the sewn patchwork as I go, aligning the drawn lines on the templates that connect the punched holes with the sewn seam lines on the fabric. Let's assume we are now going to sew the 3" Friendship Star block that has a grid dimension of 1" (remember, grid dimension does not include seam allowance). The fabric is cut and includes seam allowance on all sides of each shape. The units are created and the block is laid out, and you are ready to sew Row 1 together. To begin, sew the first two units together.

To Measure Your Work

1. Add up the number of grids you have sewn.
2. Multiply the number of grids sewn by the grid dimension.
3. Add $1/2$" for seam allowance, always.

This means two grids × 1" = 2" + $1/2$" = $2 1/2$". The first two grids of Row 1 should measure $2 1/2$" from edge to edge. If it does, great, if it does not, either the cutting or the sewing is in question. Do not continue adding grids until the first two measure $2 1/2$". When these two grids measure $2 1/2$" continue.

Continue sewing, adding the third grid or unit of Row 1 to the two already sewn. Now you have added another grid, so to measure your work, repeat steps 1, 2, and 3. Row 1, from edge to edge, should now measure $3 1/2$" (3 grids × 1" grid dimension = 3" + $1/2$" seam allowance = $3 1/2$").

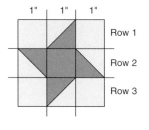

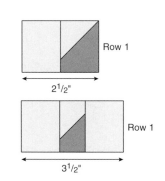

If it does, great, but if it does not, correct it. The beauty of this system is that it keeps your work accurate. If you remain faithful to this system, measuring after adding each grid, you will be able to identify where your discrepancies are because they must be in the last seam you've sewn.

To maintain the grid dimension established for the block means that you can only take $1/4$" seam allowance off each side of the accurately cut pieces, and you must take $1/4$" off, no more and no less. Additionally, the smaller the pieces you are sewing, the less tolerance for error exists.

Is this a slower way to sew? Yes! Does it ensure accuracy? Yes! Is it worth taking the time? Yes!

This is how I sew, in any scale, large or small. It is not fun to get three rows of a block all sewn and discover when you go to join the rows that the intersections don't match and the rows are different lengths, which means the outside edges of the block will be uneven. These are all unacceptable scenarios when striving to achieve quality workmanship.

I have given you the grid dimensions for the blocks that are relevant to this system. Blocks that use their templates to maintain accuracy are so noted.

Rough Cut Mock-Ups and How to Use Mirrors

Quiltmaking is divided into three areas: design, color, and workmanship. I separate design and color from workmanship, because they involve different parts of my brain. The design and color process is more emotional, free, playful, creative, and open to change. I practice, explore, and discover different skills than when I am involved with workmanship. Workmanship involves the technical process and is more deliberate, structured, focused, logical.

I use mock-ups as a design tool to compose and interview color and fabric placement in blocks or quilts before the actual cutting and sewing takes place. In the past, I rejected this idea because I was too impatient to bother with mock-ups and wanted to get right to the cutting and sewing. I was certain that mock-ups had no value whatsoever, and that diving right in was the key. As I gained experience, I learned that taking time for mock-ups or even partial mock-ups has a large value. It's not fun to get a block cut and sewn, and then upon close evaluation, critique and reflection, discover areas that could have been improved. I am a slow learner sometimes, but eventually I come around. Mock-ups are a good thing, and I have also discovered they are a fun, exciting process. Taking the time to compose and interview different colors and fabrics allows for serendipity to emerge and gives the block or quilt the time it needs to speak to us.

An important element of doing mock-ups is you do not have to be "right" the first time. You just need to put something down and then begin the process of change and refinement. You must put something, anything, down first, and then begin to improve, compose, change, and follow your heart. It is an opportunity to explore the "what if" possibilities.

What if I change red to blue, change light to dark, change floral fabric to a stripe? It is a fun, creative, challenging time and not encumbered by the sewing process.

During this design and color process I'm free to explore and play and not be concerned with how to get something sewn.

Because I usually work in a small scale I do my mock-ups in actual size without seam allowance. By working in actual size I can more accurately evaluate how color and printed fabric will look cut up, and how they relate to one another. As stated in the color and fabric chapter, color becomes darker the smaller it is cut. My 3" × 5" card with small shapes cut out helps me to read and know how prints and colors will cut up. Using a $7/8$" square of fabric in the mock-up when the finished size will be $3/8$" is deceiving, gives inaccurate information, and can defeat the entire mock-up purpose.

My experience has been that often the smallest change can make a great deal of difference. I encourage you to experiment and have fun. Once the block is ready to sew—after the design, color, and fabric choices have been made—the focus turns to the technical process. Always keep an open mind and remain flexible to change, but for the most part the color and design process is complete.

The mock-up process can also be used as a valuable learning tool to practice different color principles without ever actually sewing the block together.

I'm interested in getting as much information as possible before I cut and sew, and some blocks offer more obvious opportunity for color, value, fabric, and design manipulation than others. I can also become impatient at times. If the block design is symmetrical sometimes I only need to mock-up and compose one quadrant or one-half of the block and then use the mirrors to gain information.

Rough cut mock-ups refer to cutting shapes by eye rather than exactly. For example, if I'm making the 3" Bear's Paw block—page 75, and using templates, I simply place the templates on the desired fabric, mark dots only on the fabric through the punches, and by eye, cut from dot to dot with scissors, which will give me the finished, actual size of each shape. If the block I want to mock-up has a grid dimension, I use that information to cut my actual size shapes.

Make it easy on yourself—this should be a fun and simple exercise for gathering and evaluating information and making informed choices. I do not cut up the background fabric. Instead I move my rough-cut pieces on different fabrics, to interview different background options. I work on a small 11½" × 13½" flannel-covered foam-core board. Then using the two mirrors taped together, surround one paw on two edges, with the mirrors to view all four paws. If you want each paw to be different, the complete block would need to be composed.

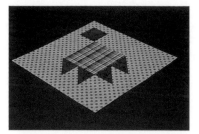

Bear's Paw mock-up

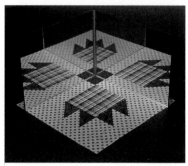

Using mirrors to view all four paws

The Pine Tree block, page 76, is another of several candidates for mock-up and mirrors. One approach is to mock-up one half of the tree by snipping, by eye or rotary cutter, all those little triangles, and place them appropriately on the desired background fabric, following the block diagram. Place the mirror so it faces the mocked up tree half and consequently reflects the whole tree.

Pine Tree block mock-up using mirrors

The Morning Star block, page 91, is another candidate and very easy to view the whole star. It is only four small diamonds. Place them appropriately on a chosen background fabric, surround them with the taped mirrors on two edges, and the mirrors will reflect the whole star.

The blocks that use this technique will be so noted. This is an exciting, challenging, useful and creative technique. Explore, have fun. It's not always where we are going or how fast we get there that matters so much as the road we take.

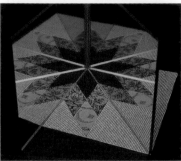

Morning Star block using mirrors

V Workmanship

Critique Criteria

The following critique criteria for evaluating and monitoring your own blocks and quilts can help as you strive for improvement. These are important issues if your objective is to achieve quality workmanship.

1. Blocks are well pressed, clean, and tidy on both front and back.
2. Blocks are square. Outside edges of block are even and straight.
3. Blocks include $1/4$" seam allowance on all outside edges and measure $3^1/2$", $4^1/2$" or $6^1/2$".
4. Value placement reflects an easy-to-read, clear design.
5. Visual texture of fabrics is interesting and varied without being too busy and chaotic.
6. All points are complete and sharp.
7. All seams match at all intersections.
8. Equality of same shapes is maintained.
9. Straight seams are straight, not wobbly.
10. Curved seams are smooth without pleats or points.
11. Triangle points (Sawtooth borders, star points, etc.) are the same height.
12. Seam allowances are trimmed/graded for 3" and 4" blocks primarily to eliminate bulk.
13. Straight grain of fabric is on outside edges of block.
14. Borders are straight and flat, not wavy or ruffled.
15. Corners of blocks and the finished quilt are 90° and square.
16. Quilting is even and balanced over the surface of the quilt.
17. If binding corners are mitered, the folds are stitched closed on both front and back.

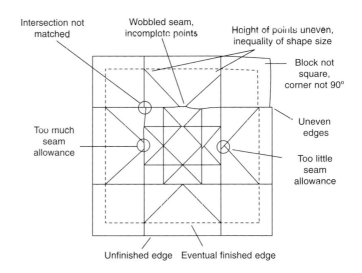

Critique and Correct Your Own Work

Eventually, we must sew to transform our ideas from paper or our mind's eye to something tangible, like a block or quilt. The technical process gives a heartbeat to our ideas. Executing each part of the process with skill and care is the distinguishing factor between ordinary and extraordinary work. To critique our own work requires an objective eye and a willingness to admit and own our errors. The goal is to achieve quality workmanship within the scope of our own personal standards.

We are each responsible for our work; improvement, not perfection, is what we are seeking. Good sewing is not about sewing perfectly each time you and your machine join forces. Good sewing is knowing how to get out of trouble when you are in it. I make mistakes daily. Being able to identify what my mistakes are, understanding what went wrong, and knowing how to correct them does not mean mistakes won't happen again. They don't happen as often, and I don't blame myself for making them. Errors are part of the quiltmaking process. Once you recognize and accept that, you begin to see mistakes in a different light. Learn from your mistakes; do what you must to clearly identify the problem and find a solution to correct it.

In my experience of working in a smaller scale, I find that the smaller the pieces the larger the sewing discrepancies become. There are basic technical sewing problems that occur repeatedly, and those are the ones I will discuss in this chapter.

One word of advice before we continue. Carefully evaluate your work as you cut and sew pieces into units, as you sew units into rows, and as you join rows into complete blocks. Remain watchful during each step of the process. Remember, it is a cumulative process, not a singular one.

To complete ten blocks and then notice they do not measure the same or the points are incomplete, is not the time to begin evaluating your work. Critiquing and correcting to achieve quality are most effective if done as you sew and go hand in hand with a deliberate, slower, focused style of working. It is slower and more time consuming, but it is worth it.

Successful quiltmaking, at any scale, depends on how well you execute each step. Individual pieces or units that are inaccurately cut and poorly sewn will result in inaccurate and poorly sewn blocks and quilts.

Quiltmaking includes a design and color process with its own detailed series of actions and a workmanship or technical process with its own skill demands. The following information is how I view the technical process as it relates to quality workmanship in sewing.

Accurate Drafting

Accurate drafting of designs and pattern shapes is critical. Check and doublecheck your drafting, numbers, measurements, and angles before cutting, and always make a sample block before cutting out the whole quilt. If you use pattern shapes from books or other sources, always measure (finished size) the two shapes' edges that will be joined to be sure they are the same size and will sew together smoothly. Never assume they are correct. A simple check with a ruler on the paper can save time and frustration when you sew. Another way is to cut up paper instead of fabric to do this preliminary checking. Accuracy and quality begins here. You must work with accurate shapes. Patchwork is like a puzzle; all the pieces must join together exactly.

Accurate Cutting

Whether you are using templates, rotary cutting or scissor cutting, if your fabric pieces are cut just $1/16$" off, over only eight pieces you have accumulated a discrepancy of $1/2$", and you haven't even sewn yet!

Rotary Cutting

I have often noticed that when using the rotary cutter and rulers, it is easy to position the ruler on the fabric edge improperly, resulting in cumulative errors that we are often unaware of. Imagine you are going to cut a 1"-wide strip from your fabric. It is pressed, folded on grain, and you have developed a straight edge. Many quilters will now position the ruler so that the 1" line on the ruler is butted up against or just touching the raw edge of the fabric, and then they make their cut. When you do this, you lose the dimension of the 1" line on the ruler every time you cut. To cut a full, maximum measurement, you must lift the ruler up and place the 1" line (or whatever the dimension you are cutting) onto the edge of the fabric—an accurate 1"-wide strip includes the 1" line on the ruler. The line should lie exactly on the edge of the fabric, don't over compensate and have fabric showing to the left. If you are using Omnigrid rulers, I am referring to the black lines, not the yellow lines.

Including the dimension line on the ruler when rotary cutting fabric accomplishes two important things. One, thread takes up space so including the line on the ruler when you cut gives the thread a place to be. Two, including the line on your ruler when you rotary cut eliminates the need for sewing with a scant $1/4$" seam allowance (whatever scant is).

Additionally, when I cut, I position my index finger on the handle of my small cutter, the blade slightly inward, getting as close to where the fabric and ruler edge meet to ensure a more accurate cut. This also prevents me from veering off to the right, away from the ruler edge and into the yardage. I usually cut only two layers of fabric at a time when rotary cutting to maintain accuracy. I use two different sizes of mats: an 18" × 24" for larger cutting and a much smaller one for subcutting. The smaller mat allows me to rotate it without moving and disturbing the fabric.

Templates

Templates are wonderful, powerful tools that give high rewards and improve our potential for both quality and custom work. Accurately made templates that include a $1/4$" seam allowance are guides for cutting angular or curved shapes from fabric. Use a substantial weight of translucent plastic that is ungridded and flat. Do not roll your template plastic. I use templates if the shape I need is a size not easily found on the ruler, if it is oddly shaped or curved, if I want to custom cut a particular area from a fabric either once or multiple times, or if I want to custom cut from a strip unit. Templates support total freedom in design. They help align two pieces of fabric for sewing by pinning at reference dots marked on the fabric pieces. They help me to monitor my sewing accuracy by reflecting sewing lines. As I sew, I place the template on the sewn units; the seam lines and lines on the template should match.

As I make templates, I use a permanent pen to mark the dots at intersections and a No. 2 pencil to note all other information. I do this because often I smear a line and/or blacken my ruler's edge with the permanent pen if it is too wet. A pencil eliminates these potential problems and allows me the flexibility to erase changes or corrections to the information on the template.

To Make a Template

1. Place a manageable size of template plastic over the shape needed. Be sure to position the plastic so that you have adequate room to add the seam allowance. You can tape the plastic in place if necessary to eliminate slipping and shifting.

2. Dot each intersection and where any line changes direction using the permanent pen. Now, even if your plastic does shift, you have established the finished size.

3. With a No. 2 pencil, align your ruler edge on the bottom of the dots so that the pencil lead is positioned at the center of the dots, and draw a line, nearly connecting the dots, leaving them open and obvious for punching or piercing. This line is the sewing line you will use to place over your work to monitor accuracy.

4. Write the identifying letter or number; block name, size, and grain line arrow on each template. These markings are very important, not only for the obvious informative reasons, but because they identify the right side of the template.

5. Cut out each template accurately by aligning the $1/4$" line of your ruler so it travels through the dots on one edge of the shape and then, using an Exacto® knife positioned next to the edge of your ruler, score the plastic. Do this on all sides of the template. Once the plastic is scored adequately it will precisely crack off leaving an exactly sized template that includes an accurate $1/4$" seam allowances on all sides of each shape. Cutting templates this way ensures that your template shapes include exactly the same seam allowance as your rotary cut pieces. You can also use a rotary cutter with an old blade, but I find the Exacto knife is easier to control.

6. Punch holes exactly at the dots, with a $1/16$" hole punch (see Source list, page 125) or place the template face down on a towel and carefully pierce the plastic at the dot with a stiletto or large needle by gently twisting, taking care not to crack the plastic. The hole should only be large enough to insert a pencil or pen to mark a dot on your fabric. The $1/8$" hole punch creates too large a hole to ensure accuracy when marking dots on fabric. These marked dots are then used as reference guides for pinning and aligning one piece of fabric onto another properly for sewing. They are also the indicators of where to stop and/or start sewing in some instances such as y-seam areas.

Before using your templates to mark and cut your fabric, do two things. First, lay your template over the pattern shape again and be sure your dots and sewing lines on the template align with the pattern shape. Second, because the shapes are interrelated, position appropriate template shapes right sides together, as if they were fabric and you were sewing. The lines, edges, and punched holes should all line up. Do not begin marking and cutting fabric until you know you have accurate templates.

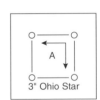

Finished template

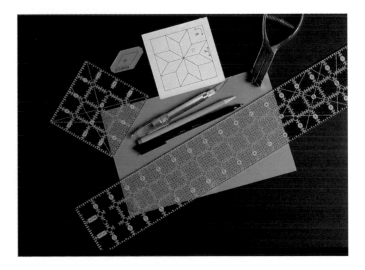

Marking and Cutting Fabric with Templates

When using templates to mark fabric, always place each template face down on the wrong side of the fabric, aligning the grain arrow with the fabric grain. Reverse templates will be placed right side up. To prevent the fabric from shifting, place the fabric on a fine-grade sandpaper board to gently hold the fabric in place while tracing around the template. Trace around the template, angling the appropriate marking tool into the edge of the template.

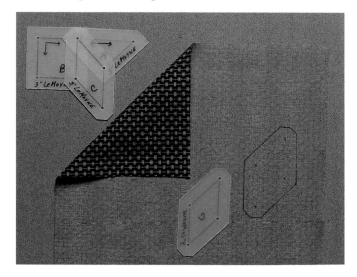

Dot each intersection through the hole (if you connected the dots you would create the sewing line). Use a pencil if possible or white pencil on darks; be wary of wet permanent pens that can bleed through to the right side of your fabric when marking dots.

Cut out each shape one at a time, using serrated-edge scissors to ensure accuracy and cutting off the drawn line. Double check accuracy by placing the template, right side up on the right side of each cut fabric shape. I do this because it is very easy (especially if making templates is new to you) to have the cut pieces be just a little larger than the template, so a few seconds now alleviates headaches and frustration later. The cut fabric shapes must be exactly the same size as the templates.

Inaccurate Cutting of Fabric

Inaccurate cutting of fabric, regardless of whether you use templates, scissors, or rotary cutter and even if you sew with an accurate $1/4"$ seam allowance can result in:

♦ Inequality among same shapes
♦ Units or blocks not measuring correctly
♦ Out-of-square or misshapen units and/or blocks
♦ Uneven edges of blocks
♦ Poorly matched intersections

Sometimes when our work is not correct, we attack, accuse, and assume it must be an inaccurate seam allowance. Next time that happens, check your cutting accuracy.

Sewing Techniques

Accurate sewing using a $1/4"$ seam allowance (the exact same seam allowance you have allowed for in your cutting), ensures successful patchwork piecing. To have all the cut pieces sew back together like a puzzle, you must take off an accurate $1/4"$ seam on all sides of all pieces, no more and no less. All machines are different. You must find how to achieve a $1/4"$ seam allowance on your machine before you begin to sew. Some quilters use tape, or a magnetic seam guide, or a $1/4"$ foot, or move their needle position. Whatever method you use, check for accuracy before you begin sewing. One way to check for accuracy is to cut two $1" \times 31/2"$ strips of any fabric, pair them right sides together with edges even and aligned, and sew down the length with an accurate $1/4"$ seam allowance (use a large stitch length in case you need to remove the stitches and retest). Open the two strip unit and press the seam allowance to one side. This unit should now measure $11/2"$ from edge to edge and also $3/4"$ from the seam to the edge in both directions.

If you get these measurements it means your cutting and sewing are accurate. If it does not measure correctly, either your cutting or sewing, or both, is in question, and you need to make the appropriate adjustment. Even if you are just a little bit off, your work will reflect the inaccuracy. For example, let's say you are sewing a 3" Bear's Paw block that has forty-five pieces and numerous seams, and you want to join it with a 3" Snowball block that has only five pieces and four seams. If you are just a little bit off, these two blocks will never be the same size because the accumulation of the "little bit off" will be greater in the block with more pieces and seams than the other. You must establish and maintain an accurate $1/4$" seam allowance. Additionally, the more pieces in the block and/or the smaller the block, the more crucial accuracy becomes and the less tolerance for error exists.

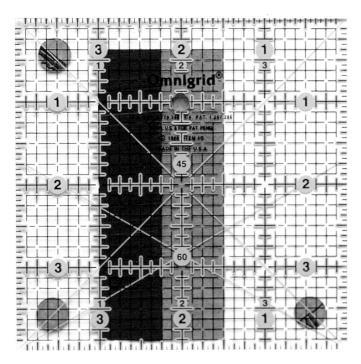

One method of checking your $1/4$" seam

Inaccurate $1/4$" Seam Allowance

Inaccurate $1/4$" seam allowances will result in:

♦ Inequality among same shapes
♦ Blocks not measuring what they should
♦ Incomplete points
♦ Poorly matched intersections
♦ Bowing of units or rows
♦ Blocks not square
♦ Uneven outside edges of blocks

Sewing Straight

Sewing straight is the most overlooked area of accurate, precise sewing. If poorly executed, this one process creates more problems than any other does. It is crucial to quality workmanship to sew straight; that is, to enter onto the fabric at $1/4$", stay at $1/4$", and exit off the fabric at $1/4$". Before you begin, be sure the pieces or rows or units you are sewing are positioned or registered onto one another correctly. Sit directly in front of your needle, clearly see your sewing path and have a sense of squareness or straightness. Look at the lines on your throat plate or the edge of your machine. As you place your fabric under the needle, the edge you are sewing should be perpendicular to the front edge of your machine. Begin to develop this sense as you continue to sew.

The two most important places when you sew are where you begin the seam and where you end the seam, especially if your line of sewing is short, because it will impact on the accuracy of pieces sewn. Unknowingly, many quilters enter onto the fabric casually, perhaps deeper or more than $1/4$". Then we straighten out and sew with a $1/4$" seam, and as we get near the end of the seam we let go of these pieces so we can pick up the next two pieces (if we are chain piecing). This results in the two pieces still under the needle sewing off unattended.

Most sewing machine feed dogs will pull your fabric to the left when you near the end of a line of sewing which results in exiting off the fabric at less than $1/4$". To remedy this problem I suggest you sew slowly, be sure you know and can clearly see the sewing path and can see the needle enter and exit the fabric exactly where you want it to. Carefully guide your work with your left hand as it goes under the needle while using a stiletto or similar tool to help keep the raw edge of your fabric pieces against whatever seam guide you are using to ensure you exit the fabric at $1/4$". Quilters often think that when they are chain piecing, one unit must follow the other closely, touching or butting next to the piece in front of it. This is not true; there is no hurry. You can actually sew with no fabric between pieces, as long as you do not lift the pressure foot high enough to disengage it. Be attentive and focus only on the pieces being sewn until the sewing needle is off the edge. Stop your machine, get the next two pieces to be sewn, position them appropriately and begin sewing again. It is not a race; do not concern yourself with anything else until the sewing needle is completely off the edge of the pieces you are sewing.

Crooked, Wavy, Unstraight Sewing

Crooked, wavy, unstraight sewing can result in:

♦ Triangle points finishing at different heights or being cut off, blunted, and incomplete
♦ Wobbly seams
♦ Inequality among same shapes
♦ Block rows bowed
♦ Out-of-square blocks

Uneven Edges

When sewing two pieces of fabric together, it is most important that their edges are even and aligned. If one edge moves away from the other, you will not be taking an accurate $1/4$" seam allowance off both. This usually happens because the edge on the bottom piece is the one that moves, the one we don't see when we sew. If you are sewing small blocks, the tiniest discrepancy here makes a huge difference. Always check to be sure edges are even before sewing.

Uneven edges can result in:

♦ Inequality between same shapes
♦ Blocks not measuring what they should
♦ Out-of-square blocks
♦ Incomplete points
♦ Points too long or too short
♦ Poorly matched intersections

Measuring and Maintaining Grid Dimension

This one element will enable you to monitor and maintain accuracy and identify what seams need adjusting. Refer to pages 19 and 22 for specifics on grid dimension and using templates to monitor your work.

Stitch Length

After testing for an accurate $1/4$" seam allowance with the two-strip technique discussed earlier on page 28, I adjust the stitch length to approximately 12–15 stitches per inch. You want to be sure the length is not so small that it becomes difficult to remove the stitches. I often change the stitch length depending on what I'm doing.

When experimenting or if I'm unsure about matching a heavily seamed intersection, I increase the stitch length or machine baste, so that I can easily remove the stitches and re-sew if needed. Another reason to slightly increase the stitch length when I am sewing a bulky, heavily seamed area is because it tends to make the seam more supple rather than rigid and stiff. I decrease the stitch length as I approach dots when doing Y-Seam Construction, page 41. This enables me to sew very close to the appropriate dots without sewing into them. Another area where I would decrease my stitch length is when pressing a seam open, which creates a potential opportunity for the thread to show.

Sewing Thread, Type and Color

I use 100 percent cotton DMC Machine Embroidery thread 50/2 in the top and bobbin of my machine for all my sewing. This is a fine, thin thread, and it takes up less space, which results in flatter seams. This thread also leaves less fluff under your throat plate than the larger spools of cotton thread, and you will be able to significantly increase the amount of thread on the bobbin.

I use a medium or muddy tan or gray colored thread, which blends into most fabrics. Matching color is not as important as blending or camouflaging. You do not want to see the thread from the right side of the work. When in doubt, choose a darker thread color in relation to the fabric. If I were working in black and white, for instance, I would choose black thread. Blocks with open seams or numerous seams intersecting (sixteen in a Split-Diamond LeMoyne Star block) create more opportunity for thread to show, so be aware and attentive to thread color and stitch length.

Noteworthy

Even when I think I'm being most careful, there are times when I can see little dots of light thread showing from the right side of my block. When this happens, I gently, precisely and carefully, rub or touch the thread with a pencil lead, which will take away the lightness and make it less noticeable to the eye. It is tempting to use a permanent marker, but I always try the pencil first. If that does not do the trick, then and only then do I use a permanent marker to "custom dye" the thread. Be sure the marker is on the dry side instead of wet because it will bleed to other areas and ruin the work.

Feeding Fabric under the Needle Smoothly

♦ Sew on a folded scrap of fabric first, and then feed your "real" pieces behind the scrap. When you have fed all your pieces under the needle, stop your machine with the needle down but do not lift your pressure foot up. Cut off your leader scrap piece, bring it to the needle and sew on it again, and then cut your "real" pieces off. As a result, you are not pulling your work out from the machine to clip threads which leaves little thread tails all over the back of your block and at the ends of seams. Also there are no threads on the floor, resulting in a neater work area.

Whenever you are sewing edge to edge, your machine will take on small pieces much easier if it is already sewing on the scrap, and you will not be lifting your pressure foot up and down. If you are doing y-seam construction, page 41, or if you do not use a scrap leader to begin sewing, you will need to hold the top and bobbin threads when you begin sewing, or you will get a bobbin bulge on the back of your work. If this happens, remove it and start over.

♦ Use the stiletto as an extension of your hand to help guide pieces of fabric under the needle straight and to keep the edges against whatever seam guide you use. A wooden skewer, toothpick, seam ripper, or large pin also work well.

♦ A straight stitch throat plate (the one with the tiny round hole) is a must if working small because it lessens the opportunity for fabric to be "eaten." It is also a must when machine quilting because it will result in straight, nicer looking stitches. For obvious reasons the needle must be kept in the center position when using the straight stitch throat plate. The larger opening on the zigzag throat plate is a greater opportunity for fabric to get shoved into.

♦ Change your sewing machine needle, clean under the throat plate, and oil appropriately after every fifteen to twenty hours of sewing or at least after completing each project. You'll be amazed at how well your machine will perform if you treat it with kindness.

Noteworthy

I have been asked why I do not use two scrap pieces, one to begin with and one to end with. When I tried using two I was always looking for the second scrap. When you work with only one scrap piece you always know where it is!

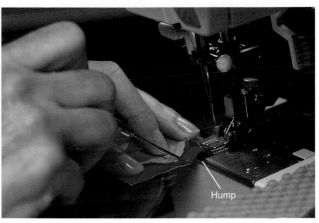

Hump created as fabric feeds under presser foot.

♦ When chain piecing, you may find your machine skews or shifts the two pieces of fabric being sewn. What is happening is your machine is pushing the top layer or piece off the bottom layer because the feed dogs are grabbing only the bottom piece. This becomes very obvious and apparent especially when sewing small pieces. You can tell this is happening because you will see a hump created just as you feed or push the fabric under the pressure foot when chain piecing. To remedy this, when I chain piece, rather than pushing my pieces under the foot, I slightly lift my presser foot up (do not raise it all the way up and disengage it), position my work under the foot and in front of the needle, lower the foot and continue to sew. This results in more successful sewing and less skewing because it enables your machine to grab both pieces simultaneously. The foot applies pressure on the work from the top as the feeddogs grab from the bottom. Also, when chain piecing, it is not necessary that one unit or piece of fabric touch the one in front of it. You can actually sew without fabric between the pieces being chained as long as the presser foot is not completely lifted and disengaged. It is more important to sew off the fabric edge, stop sewing, pick up the next pieces, lift the pressure foot slightly, position the fabric appropriately under the foot, lower the foot and continue chaining. Yes, this takes a little more time, but remember, it is not a race. Quality workmanship takes time.

Removing Stitches

When it becomes necessary to remove stitches and re-sew, do so carefully so as not to distress, tear or fray your fabric. The seam ripper is an invaluable, helpful, and important tool but should be used carefully, properly, and with respect. Never "rip" out stitches. Instead, when you have a line of stitches that need to be removed, cut every third or fourth stitch, turn your work over, and lift that interlocking thread. It will easily release, and the two pieces will separate.

Careful removal of inappropriate stitches will enable you to reposition and resew the pieces over and over (if necessary) without having to dispose of them and recut.

Pinning

I use 1¼" long × .50mm IBC Super Fine Silk Pins #5004. They are long, fine, thin pins without glass heads. The pins slide into fabric easily with little or no distortion on the edge of the fabric. This results in a flatter piece for the machine to sew. I sew over all my pins successfully without breaking needles or harming my machine because the combination of slow sewing and fine pins allows the machine needle to slide in front of or behind the pins as it sews. Speed or fast sewing over pins is what breaks sewing machine needles.

I use pins to secure intersections, match points (alignment pin), ease areas of fullness, keep outside edges even, match dots (which helps position one piece onto another properly), and sometimes to simply transport small work to the machine. I use pins whenever it helps my work and benefits my sewing.

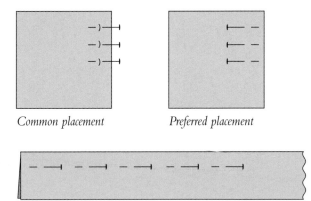

Common placement   Preferred placement

Parallel placement on narrow strip

Most quilters position their pins perpendicular to the edge, with pin heads to the right as the fabric goes under the needle. This positioning creates humps, bumps, and distortion in the path of your sewing machine needle as you sew. I usually position the pin heads to the left which creates a flatter, smoother path for your sewing machine to follow.

When sewing narrow strips of fabric together or when adding borders onto a quilt or sashing on blocks, place pins parallel to the edge and draw them out as you approach them. This creates much less distortion than a perpendicular pin placement.

Pressing

Effective pressing is setting a seam with heat, not pressure or weight. Use a dry iron and lift and place the iron onto the appropriate areas to be pressed instead of sliding the iron around. I prefer a soft surface, like an ironing board covered with a towel. Steam dampens the fabric, which can make it stretch, distort, pleat, and pucker. I use steam or custom dampening only when blocking. Move the iron in the direction of the fabric grain instead of an angle to prevent any distortion.

Before pressing the seam allowance open or in any one particular direction, I set the seam first by placing the iron on the stitching line just sewn. This relaxes the thread, eases in any fullness, and nestles the stitches into the fabric. You will find if you do this, your work will be flatter, smoother, more square and accurate. Setting the seam or opening a seam is the only time I press from the wrong side of the fabric.

I press seams all to one side or sometimes open and occasionally I collapse them. Ideally, you want to plan and create opposing seams for easy matching of intersections and to aid in maintaining squareness. If a seam allowance needs to be re-directed, you must first re-set the seam as discussed earlier, and then press it in the new direction.

Pieces will also fit together much easier if each seam is pressed before it is sewn over. Pressing each seam will help give you the maximum measurement. I use my hands and fingers to arrange, manipulate, and prepare the area to be pressed and then place the iron in that area. If you have cut and sewn accurately, there is no need to smooth and stretch the fabric outward toward the edges.

Pressing can either distort your work or help you reshape it. The direction seam allowances are pressed can also make a large difference in how the piecing looks from the right side of the block. Pressing seams in one direction could round out a point in some instances, or pressing in the opposite direction could sharpen the point, and opening a seam could improve it even more and distribute the bulk. Poor pressing can distort beautiful piecing. When opening a seam, an alternative to setting the seam with the iron is to first open the seam with your hands by running a fingernail down the seam while supporting it with the opposite hand. When you do this you will feel the two fabrics separate and the stitches relax.

A good open seam requires the two fabrics to separate down to the thread. After opening the seam with your hands, use the iron and press from the back first and then from the right side.

Collapsing the seams helps to distribute and reduce bulk and can be done on simple four-seam intersections. To collapse a seam, remove (do not cut) the vertical stitches in the seam allowance at the intersection, one at a time, to the last horizontal line of stitching on both pieces. With your hands, arrange the seam allowance in opposite directions and then press.

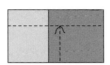

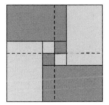

Blocking

Carefully blocking units, rows, or blocks bring them to their appropriate size and shape if there is a slight discrepancy. Remember, fabric is fluid and quality cotton is forgiving and can be arranged and manipulated, if necessary. To block your work, you need to have a gridded mat on your ironing board or draw the appropriate size square on a piece of muslin (including seam allowance). During the sewing process it is important that units and rows maintain their correct grid dimension and shape. To block rows and units, I press them, place a ruler over the piece and measure, evaluate the shape, and rearrange it if only a slight adjustment needs to be made.

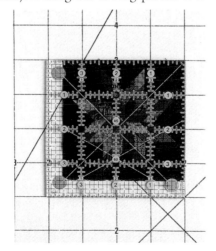

Pin in place if necessary, place the ruler over it again, then weight it with a book and let it cool in place before moving it. Take care to maintain a sense of squareness throughout the sewing process. Misshapen units and rows are going to create misshapen blocks.

To block a completed block, place it on the drawn muslin square or gridded mat and steam press the block while gently encouraging the edges outward to meet the drawn guidelines or patting and "scooching" the edges inward to meet them. Pin it in place, put a square ruler on top of the block, then place a book or weight on it and let it cool before moving it. Final pressing from the top on a soft surface allows the seam allowances to sink into the towel for a flatter look and eliminates the possibility of ridges forming from the seam allowances as well.

To Prevent Multiple Strip Units From Bowing or Curving

♦ Press each seam after adding each strip rather than sewing them all together and then pressing.
♦ Cut strips on the length grain and cut shorter strips.
♦ Press in a perpendicular direction to the stitching line.

Straight strip units ensure easier cutting and sewing of segments and squarer blocks.

Trimming and Grading Seam Allowances

The blocks and projects in this book all use a $1/4$" seam allowance. If you are doing a 3" block, with fifty pieces, and all the pieces have a $1/4$" seam allowance on all their sides, you can imagine the bulk that accumulates. To alleviate and distribute the bulk, I trim seams to a generous $1/8$". I trim whether the seam is open or pressed in one direction. If the seam is pressed open, trim up one side, then the other. Often I'm asked why not trim both the seam allowances at the same time before opening, and my answer is that it is much easier to trim an open seam than it is to open an already trimmed seam. Yes, it takes a little more time, but it is well worth it. Creating a well sewn, flat, small block requires trimmed seam allowances.

Grading seams is also an option anytime and is preferred when you have a heavily seamed intersection. Grading creates a slope rather than a step that is created by a trimmed seam, and creates a flatter intersection. To grade a seam, you will be looking at the back or wrong side of the work. Trim the seam allowance that is on top and closest to you more than the seam allowance underneath. Some sewers know how to slant

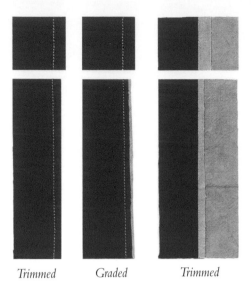

Trimmed   *Graded*   *Trimmed*

their scissors and grade a seam in one cut. Because I do not know how to do that, I must make two cuts, which takes twice the time. I trim or grade all seams because it eliminates bulk and makes quilting easier, but you may find larger blocks do not need it.

It often depends on the purpose of the quilt and the size of the pieces. Small work demands trimmed or graded seams to lie flat and view well. Some guidelines to follow are:

♦ Use serrated-edge scissors that grab the fabric rather than let it slip and be miscut.

♦ Do not trim or grade too much because the seam allowance will stand straight up rather than press to one side or the other. This condition creates problems when quilting because the seam allowance will wiggle from one side of the seam to the other.

♦ Make certain your work is correct before trimming. If you trim or grade the seam and then discover you need to remove stitches and re-sew, your seam allowance will have been distorted and changed, which makes re-sewing more difficult. This is just one of many reasons why it is so important to maintain grid dimension and critique and correct your work before trimming or grading. If you do trim and then discover you need to remove stitches and re-sew, you can remove the appropriate stitches and measure over from the opposite edge the grid dimension plus $1/4$" and draw a sewing line. If you are using templates and have dots on your fabric, just connect the dots to create your sewing line.

♦ When your quilt block is complete, it should have a $1/4$" seam allowance on all sides. Trimming up or squaring up is not a way to correct problems or bring your work to the right size. Trimming up should only create straight edges and remove thread tails.

VI Construction Techniques

There are always many roads that lead to the same place. This is also true of sewing techniques and methods available to accomplish a specific sewing task. The techniques and methods described here work for me and are based on precision, accuracy, and efficiency, as well as the type of specific task. I never compromise accuracy for speed. I always try to customize my techniques to meet the needs of the specific task.

Half-Square Triangles

Individual right angle triangles and triangle units for the blocks in this book are cut and sewn in several different ways, depending on their size, straight grain placement, and how many are needed of a particular fabric. Each block specifies which method I felt was the most successful in each individual case, but you always have the option of choosing your own.

Individual Half-Square Triangles

Individual half-square or right-angle triangles are used in many patchwork blocks and are simply created by cutting a square in half diagonally, which results in the two short sides of the triangles being on the straight grain and the one longer leg being on the bias grain. Two of these triangles sewn together create a square.

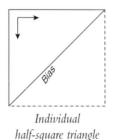

Individual half-square triangle

To cut individual half-square triangles that include $1/4$" seam allowance, simply determine the finished length of the short side of the triangle needed. Add $7/8$" to that number, cut a square that size, then sub-cut the square in half diagonally to create two half-square triangles that now include $1/4$"

seam allowance on all three sides. It is extremely important when rotary cutting these triangles that they be accurate.

Place the edge of the ruler on the square exactly corner to corner and cut with the rotary cutter. The blade does not take up space so there is no need to back up the ruler edge to accommodate the blade.

To sew individual triangles together to form a square, (half-square triangle unit), pair two triangles, right sides together, aligning all three edges, and sew down the long bias edge. To maintain an accurate $1/4$" seam allowance from point to point and be able to chain piece, stop sewing with the needle down about a $1/16$" from the edge, lift the foot and position the next pair of triangles under the foot, slightly overlapping the points which creates stability while continuing to

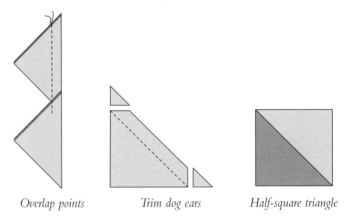

Overlap points *Trim dog ears* *Half-square triangle*

sew. Separate the chain of triangles by snipping the threads in between. Press the stitches, trim off the dog-ears (the excess that extends beyond the end of the seam), then open the piece for final pressing. Trimming in this manner will create a square half-square triangle unit.

Half-Square Triangle Unit

A half-square triangle unit is simply a square composed of two different colored right angle triangles that are sewn together to create a square. This type of unit can be created in a variety of ways. The following are techniques I use most often to create half-square triangles.

Noteworthy

OVERSIZE AND CUSTOM CUT TECHNIQUE is self-explanatory. A pieced unit is created deliberately larger than needed and then the exact, or required, size unit is cut from it. The advantages are that it is stress-free, the required size unit is cut exactly and precisely, and the seam allowances are already pressed and trimmed. Additionally, this technique can be used in a variety of instances such as half-square triangles, quarter-square triangles, four 45° diamond units, and four-patches, to name a few. I use this technique most often when working in a small scale, but it is not limited to that scale.

For example, let's say I want to create a 1" finished half-square triangle unit. Rather than cutting a $1^7/_8$" square (finished size plus $^7/_8$") of two fabrics, cutting them in half diagonally and sewing two of the triangles back together to result in a $1^1/_2$" half-square triangle unit (1" plus seam allowance) as described earlier, you would increase the size of the $1^7/_8$" square to perhaps $2^1/_4$" square. The increase is up to you; there is no specific recipe, just larger.

The larger square results in a larger unit from which to custom cut the exact desired size unit. How to accurately custom cut an exact sized unit from an oversized unit will be explained as each type of unit is introduced.

Stitched Grid Technique

Stitched grid technique is based on the add $^7/_8$" to the finished size of the half-square-triangle units premise. I do this technique sparingly for blocks like Bear's Paw, when I need a few units from the same two fabrics. The following technique yields eight individual half-square-triangle units at a time.

1. Determine the finished size of the desired half-square triangle unit.
2. Add $^7/_8$" to this number, then double it. (i.e., 1" finished unit + $^7/_8$" = $1^7/_8$" × 2 = $3^3/_4$" square.)
3. Cut a $3^3/_4$" square from the two desired fabrics. Place them right sides together and draw lines on the light fabric from corner to corner in both directions and horizontally and vertically. These drawn lines are eventual cutting lines.
4. Sew $^1/_4$" on both sides of the drawn diagonal lines only.
5. Cut on all drawn lines to yield eight segments.
6. Press the seams open and trim. Each unit will measure $1^1/_2$" square if accurately cut and sewn.

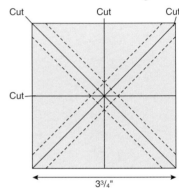

You always have the option of exercising the Oversize and Custom Cut technique (I usually do) by increasing the size of the two original squares by $^3/_4$", proceeding as stated and then custom cut the exact size desired from the oversized units (See Square-to-Square Technique, page 38, for cutting information).

$1^1/_2$"

Bias Strip Technique

This is an accurate technique that adapts beautifully to any scale. I first became aware of this technique from Marsha McCloskey. Although I only sew two strips together rather than multiple strips and sub-cut units from the bias strips in a little different manner, the concept is the same. Bias strips are sewn together, the seam allowances are carefully pressed open and trimmed, and then squares of a desired size are sub-cut from the sewn bias strips which result in the squares having straight grain on their four outside edges. This technique eliminates the need to press and trim each individual unit and the possibility of distortion. To determine the width to cut the bias strips, add ¹/₂" to the cut size of the half-square triangle unit. This is a generous cut.

1. Pair two fabrics, right sides together and press.
2. Develop a 45° angle and cut the needed width and number of bias strips required.
3. Sew the paired bias strips down their length with a ¹/₄" seam allowance. Press the stitches, press the seam open and trim.
4. To cut the desired size half-square triangle units from the bias strips you need to first establish a 45° angle on one end. Now rotate the strip unit, and cut slices the width of the cut size half-square triangle unit. The key to an accurate angle and slices is to keep the 45° line of the ruler placed on the seam of the strip unit, not the edges.

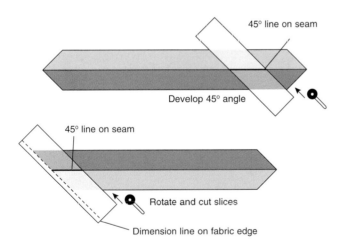

When you are cutting slices, you must keep both the 45° line of the ruler on the seam and the cut dimension line of the ruler on the edge of the fabric. If you cannot align both, this means the angle has tipped off and you need to re-establish it. This is not an uncommon thing to have happen and could occur as often as every third slice. If the 45° line of the ruler is not on the seam when you cut, you may not be cutting a true 45° angled slice. Poorly angled slices result in poorly cut half-square triangle units and inequality between the two triangles will occur.

5. To cut squares from the slices, first align a square ruler with its 45° line on the diagonal seam of the slice so that the corner of the square ruler is aligned with the top of the diagonal seam where the two triangles meet. Place the top edge of the ruler at the top edge of the slice, the chosen square dimension line is at the bottom of the slice, and cut.

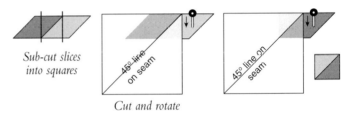

Cut and rotate

6. Rotate the slice and realign the ruler similarly so the 45° line of the square ruler is on the diagonal seam, the top edge of the ruler is at the top edge of the slice, and the dimension line is at the bottom of the slice, and cut.

Noteworthy

Rather than roll the cutter towards the corner seam where the bulk is and risk the fabric moving under the ruler, cut the corner first by pressing downward with the cutter, then roll the blade toward yourself.

Square-to-Square Technique

Square-to-square technique creates individual half-square triangle units and is successful, simple, and accurate when you need only one or two units each from a variety of fabrics and colors like the Pine Tree block. Let's say you want to create a 1" finished half-square triangle unit.

1. Cut two $1^1/_2$" squares (1" plus $^1/_2$") of two chosen fabrics. Draw a diagonal line on the wrong side of the lightest fabric. Pair both squares, right sides together, and sew on this line.

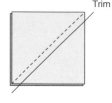

2. Trim to within $^1/_4$" of the stitches, press seam open, and trim again to a generous $^1/_8$". If making larger units, press seam allowance to the darker fabric.

3. Unit is now $1^1/_2$" square if cut and sewn accurately.

4. When working small, I always use oversized squares and custom cut my desired units from them using a square ruler with a 45° line. You could also eliminate the need to draw a line (oversized units only) by using the Sticky Note Technique—page 38.

5. Position the ruler on the oversized square so that the 45° line is on the seam and there is fabric visible beyond the $1^1/_2$" lines on all four sides. Trim the first two sides, rotate unit, and trim again as shown.

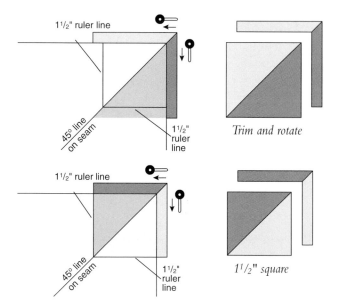

Trim and rotate

$1^1/_2$" square

Sticky Note Technique

When sewing oversized half-square triangles using the Square-to-Square technique as in the Pine Tree block, page 76, you can eliminate the need to draw a sewing line by positioning the sticky edge of a sticky note to your machine, lining it up with the center of the needle outward towards you. Use a ruler to be sure it is straight. Align the paired squares to be sewn diagonally so that both their corner points are always on the edge of the sticky note. This will ensure you are sewing diagonally from one corner to the other.

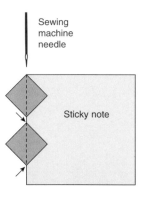

Quarter-Square Triangle Units

Quarter-square triangles are made from a square of fabric that is cut into quarters diagonally, which places the straight of grain on the longest side of the triangle.

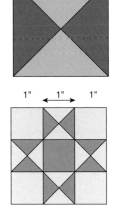

1"   1"   1"

3" finished

To know what size to cut the squares, determine the finished length of the longest side of the triangle and add $1\frac{1}{4}$". For example, if the finished length of the long leg of the triangle is 1" plus $1\frac{1}{4}$" equals $2\frac{1}{4}$" square.

1. Cutting the $2\frac{1}{4}$" square into quarters is a simple task but must be done accurately to maintain equality among the shapes. Place your ruler edge diagonally on the square, exactly through both corners. Firmly stabilize the ruler with your hands so it does not move while cutting. Cut with your rotary cutter angled slightly so the blade cuts as close to the ruler edge as possible.

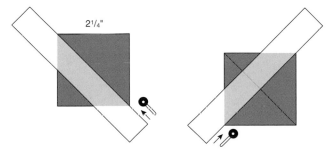

$2\frac{1}{4}$"

2. Carefully lift the ruler and reposition its edge through the two opposite corners.
3. If the triangles do move when you reposition the ruler you can easily cut them one at a time. Take your square or long ruler and position it on the individual triangles so that the top edge of the ruler is on the top edge of the triangle and the side edge of the ruler is aligned from the top edge and through the point.

 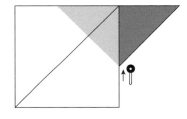

4. Refer to the Ohio Star—page 51 to see how quarter-square triangles are constructed.

Noteworthy

When making quarter-square triangle units, I oversize the original square, then when the triangles are sewn together to create a unit, I custom cut the exact size I need from the larger unit. Because custom cutting this type of unit is dependent upon coming from the center intersection out toward all four edges one-half of the eventual cut size, it is more simply done if the cut size of the unit needed is divisible by two. If it is not, make a square from template plastic the cut size needed, draw lines corner to corner in both directions to align with the center intersection and diagonal seams, place it on the larger unit, and custom cut.

For example, to custom cut a $1\frac{1}{2}$" square from a larger quarter-square triangle, position the square ruler so that the $\frac{3}{4}$" (half of $1\frac{1}{2}$") intersection is on the center intersection of the unit, which places the corner of the ruler where the two different fabrics join, and the 45° line is on one diagonal seam. At the same time be sure the other diagonal seam runs corner to corner through the $\frac{1}{8}$" grid squares on the ruler.

When all three alignment perspectives are in place, cut the side and top edge. Rotate the segment, reposition the square ruler and make the final two cuts. It is important to align the ruler as described to create equality among the four triangles and have the seams split the four corners exactly.

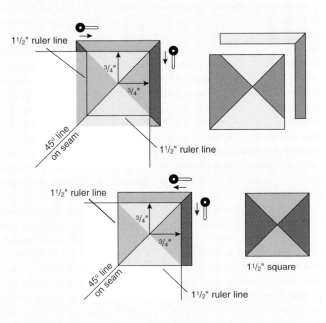

Double Half-Square Triangle Units

Although this unit is composed of three triangles, it will be constructed using a rectangle and two squares.

This unit is often called a Flying Geese unit. I first became aware of this technique from the book *Quilts! Quilts! Quilts!!!* by Diana McClun and Laura Nownes. I use this technique because it is easy to cut and there is less chance for error because there are no exposed bias edges to deal with. Blocks in this book using this technique are Dutchman's Puzzle—page 54, Jack-In-the-Box—page 65, Carpenter's Wheel Variation—page 86, Rising Star and Square—page 59, and Arizona—page 63. Each block will give specific cutting and sewing directions. For explanation purposes, the following will create star points, although you can change the configuration by simply changing the direction of the diagonal seams and/or the value placement.

Flying Geese

Star Points

Jack-in-the-Box/ Carpenter's Wheel Variation

1. Cut a rectangle and two squares.
2. Draw a diagonal line on the wrong side of each square.

3. Place one square onto one end of the rectangle, right sides together, being sure all appropriate edges are aligned, and sew just on the scrap side of the line. The scrap side is the side that gets trimmed away. My experience when doing this technique has been that if I sew directly on the line, the square's corner does not meet the rectangle's corner exactly. Also, thread takes up space, so sewing on the scrap side of the line gives a small amount of space back and makes the two corners meet more comfortably.

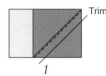

1   *2*   *3*

4. Bring the square's corner over the stitching to the rectangle's corner. If the corners meet comfortably and to your standards, trim away the square's scrap triangle to within ¹/₈" of the stitches, leaving the rectangle in place.

5. After trimming, press toward the newly added triangle.
6. Add the second square at the other end and sew as described in steps 3 and 4. The direction of the second diagonal could change depending on what block you are doing.

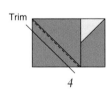

4   *5*   *6*

Sew and Flip Technique

This technique used in the center of Rising Star and Square—page 59, Bow Ties—page 55, and Arizona—page 63, is constructed using the same concept as the double half-square triangle wherein you will use all squares, no triangles, sew on the scrap side of the drawn line, trim the scrap triangle away, and bring one corner to the other corner.

Notice that the larger square that ends up holding the four corner triangles and becomes the square on point remains in place, as the rectangle does in the double half-square triangle, for the same reason.

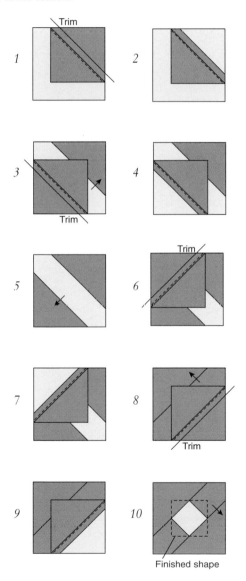

Y-Seam Construction

This type of seam construction is needed when three seams meet in one place, which makes it necessary to leave the seam allowances free to press a flat, smooth intersection. This kind of sewing is not difficult, but it is slower and choppy, rather than continuous and smooth like chain piecing. You will need to remove the work from the machine and reposition often. You just need to change your mindset and resign yourself to this type of slower sewing.

I often find the most beautiful blocks requiring some y-seaming like Castle Wall—page 100, LeMoyne Star—page 90, and Cornucopia—page 95, require templates. Punching holes in the templates appropriately enables you to mark reference dots on your fabric, which will indicate the seam allowance area. If you stitch one thread into the seam allowance area when y-seaming, you will create a pucker. I have found that if you stop sewing and backstitch just before entering the dot, you will create a successful, flat, smooth intersection every time. You must, however, stitch as close to the dot as possible ($1/16$" to $1/32$") to not leave an obvious hole. I dial my stitch length smaller as I approach the dot but never enter the needle into the dot.

Always identify what dots are y-seam areas and which are not. Do not stop at dots that are not y-seam areas and backstitch; instead sew off the edge. Pinning and matching dots also helps to align and register the pieces onto each other for sewing and helps to identify the sewing path (remember if you connect the dots, that is your sewing line). When possible, I always arrange my pieces so that I begin at the edge and sew to the dot and backstitch rather than begin at the dot.

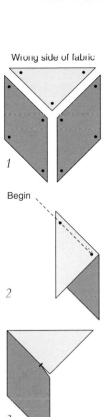
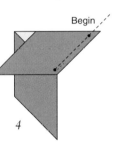
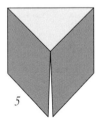
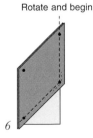
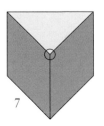

Strip Piecing

Strip piecing is used in patchwork in obvious ways, such as with equal width strips, creating four-patches or nine-patches or fracturing one diamond into four or more diamonds. There are also times when you might sew strips together of unequal widths and use a template to cut out shapes. Some of the blocks that use strip piecing are Interlocking Square—page 66, Sawtooth Double Nine-Patch—page 85, Morning Star—page 91, Basket—page 64, Cornucopia—page 95 and Mississippi Queen—page 56. Accurately sewing strips together to create straight, unbowed strip units is essential to creating accurate square units and blocks.

1. Cut strips on the length grain and work with shorter strip lengths to avoid stretch. Fabric must be folded on grain to avoid bends at the folds when cutting the strips.

2. Press carefully (see Pressing, page 32) after adding each strip and maintain straightness by aligning the edge of the strip unit to a drawn line or grid line at the ironing board.

3. Be sure your tension and/or stitch length is not so tight that it draws up the strips slightly. If you begin with 12" strips, the strip unit should maintain that length.

4. If opening the seams, use a small stitch length and a well-camouflaged thread color.

5. When adding strips, sew from the same end rather than opposite ends. Also, when joining strips to create fractured 45° diamonds, offset the strips by their width to avoid waste.

6. Focus on sewing straight and maintaining the grid dimension after adding each strip to assure the unit is the exact width required.

7. When sub-cutting the strip units into segments, maintain the chosen angle (90° or 45°), keep them straight, and re-establish the chosen angle you are cutting after three or four cuts. Poorly cut segments will make crooked units, blocks and quilts.

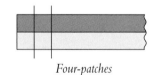

Four-patches

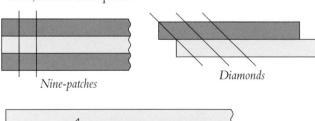

Nine-patches

Diamonds

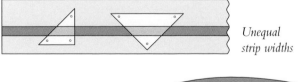

Unequal strip widths

Poorly sewn and pressed strip unit

Metal Bias Bars

Metal bias bars come in a variety of widths and can be used with straight or bias grain fabric strips, depending upon their purpose. In this book either $^1/_8$" or $^1/_4$" metal bars will be used with bias fabric to create stems, vines, or basket handles. The blocks that use these bars are Basket—page 64, Postage Stamp Basket—page 73, North Carolina Lily—page 101, and Heart and Leaf Lyre—page 82. Each relevant block will give specific bar width and fabric cutting information. You will then be referred to the instructions that follow to create the bias.

1. Cut fabric strips $^7/_8$" wide when using the $^1/_8$" bar and 1" wide when using the $^1/_4$" bar.

2. Fold the bias strips wrong sides together and gently press to create a fold, keeping the iron away from the bias edges.

3. Sew $^1/_4$" from the raw edges if you are using the $^1/_8$" bar. Sew $^1/_4$" from the fold if you are using the $^1/_4$" bar.

4. After sewing a few inches, insert the appropriate bar to be sure it fits well. The bar should fit snugly, not too loose. Sew with small stitches.

5. When sewing is complete, insert the bar, and trim the seam allowance to slightly less than $^1/_8$" with the rotary cutter and move the seam to the back of the bar, making sure no seam allowance shows from the right side.

6. With metal bar still inserted, dampen and press the seam allowance all to one side until dry, being careful not to scorch the fabric. Let the bar and fabric cool in place before removing the bar or the bias will become rounded and difficult to appliqué in place. A flat bias piece with sharply creased edges is desired.

7. Once bias is created, apply to the appropriate block per pattern instructions.

Partial Seaming

This technique is explained and used in the Interlocking Square block only—page 67, Step 4.

English Paper Piecing

This technique uses freezer paper, cut the finished size of the desired shape to stabilize the fabric as the seam allowance is brought over the edge and thread basted in place. The fabric seam allowance is thread basted over the paper edge rather than glued in place because it would be difficult to hand stitch the two edges together through the glue. The shapes are joined to each other by hand, using an overcast stitch. Blocks using this technique are Tumbling Blocks—page 81, created from nine diamonds, and Grandmother's Flower Garden—page 82, created from nineteen hexagons. Although the shapes are different for each block, the technique is the same. Each block will refer you to the following instructions.

1. Trace and cut out the appropriate shapes from the dull side of freezer paper. Be sure all the shapes are equal in size for ease of matching and sewing.

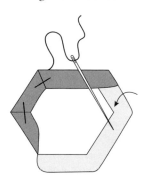

2. Press the freezer paper shapes, shiny side down onto the wrong side of the appropriate fabrics, leaving adequate space between for seam allowance.

3. Cut out each shape, allowing a $^3/_{16}$" seam allowance from the paper edge. If doing the 3" block, a slightly less seam is needed.

4. Thread a needle with light weight thread and with the paper facing you, bring the fabric seam allowance over the paper edge, fingerpress firmly, and baste in place with small stitches. Use your needle as a tool to create sharper corners by laying the needle at the paper's edge to give the fabric a more rigid edge to fold over.

5. Lay out the shapes to create the appropriate design.

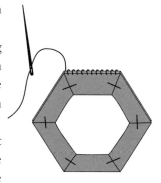

Assemble in numerical order

6. As shown, place the first two related shapes right sides together. Thread a needle and join the two edges by hand using a tiny overcast stitch and matching the thread color to the fabric.

Give a slight tug after each stitch so the stitches nestle into the fabric rather than lie on the surface. Check how your stitches look from the front often. Sew in the direction of the arrows, adding each shape in numerical order.

7. The Tumbling blocks are created by sewing three separate cubes together, then joining the cubes to complete the block.

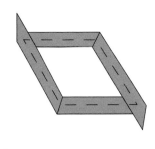

8. The Grandmother's Flower Garden is created by adding one hexagon at a time, in numerical order, in a clockwise direction.

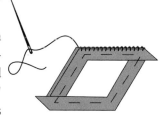

9. Place the completed unit on a variety of background fabrics to find the best one and then cut a 4", 5", or 7" square. Fold and lightly press horizontally and vertically to determine the center.

Push a pin through the center of the completed fabric design and then into the center of the background square. Align the design squarely using the fold lines as guidelines and hold in place using Hot Tape.

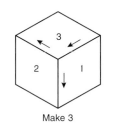

Make 3

10. Appliqué the design in place, matching the thread to the fabric. Cut out the background fabric behind the design to within $^3/_{16}$" to $^1/_4$" of the appliqué stitches.

11. Remove all the basting; carefully loosen the freezer paper and remove it with tweezers.

12. Place the block face down on a soft surface and press. Trim the background square to $3^1/_2$", $4^1/_2$" or $6^1/_2$".

Hand Appliqué

There are three blocks using hand appliqué: Sue and Bill—page 84, Heart and Leaf Lyre—page 82, and my own Leaf Design—page 83. Regardless of what block you choose to do, the preparation of the individual shapes and the background square is the same, and the block instructions will refer you to the following information.

Shape preparation

1. From the appropriate block pattern, trace all the shapes onto the dull side of freezer paper. Cut out the shapes, cutting on the line consistently.

2. Press each paper shape, shiny side down on the wrong side of each fabric. Leave room around each shape for seam allowance. Place the shapes on the bias unless the fabric print dictates otherwise.

3. Apply the GluTube to both the fabric and paper edge about $1/8$" to $3/16$". Let the glue dry; it will remain tacky.

4. Cut out each shape, allowing the $1/8$" to $3/16$" seam allowance. Too much seam allowance will be bulky, too little will not be secure.

5. With paper facing you, bring the fabric seam allowance over the paper edge. Place the prepared shapes in a zippered bag.

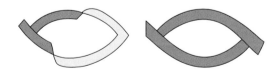

Background preparation

1. Cut a 4", 5", or 7" square from chosen background fabric. Fold and lightly press into quarters horizontally and vertically to identify center and help with placement. The Leaf Design—page 83, requires diagonally pressing for placement guidelines. It is also helpful to indicate the finished block size so you keep the shapes within the design area. If you use a washout marker, do not press the block again until you have removed the markings.

2. Place the background square over the block pattern and lightly make placement markings. For leaves I make the tip marks, for the heart I make the two humps and the bottom tip, etc. The least amount of markings the better. If only a quarter of the design is given, use the fold lines for placement, make the markings and rotate. If you are using a dark background, or want to reverse the direction of the design, or if you have difficulty seeing it through your background fabric, use a light box or tape the design to a window. Darkening the lines is always an option.

3. If you are making the Heart and Leaf Lyre—page 82, you will apply the bias vine first using Roxanne's Glue-Baste-It and appliqué both edges in place, add the leaves, then add the heart. For the Leaf Design, apply the leaves, then the center circles. For Sue and Bill, apply the shapes in numerical order.

4. Hot Tape the shapes to the background as you go and appliqué in place. Use a thread color that matches the appliqué fabric exactly, not the background fabric.

5. Remove the paper from the back of the completed block by carefully cutting the background fabric just enough to expose and remove the paper shape. Tweezers are helpful. For Sue and Bill, you can remove the paper from the front on those shapes that have an exposed edge.

6. Trim the background square to $3^1/2$", $4^1/2$", or $6^1/2$".

7. Remove any exposed markings; place the block face down on a soft surface and press from the back.

Very Narrow Borders ($^1/_8$")

Very narrow borders give unexpected sparkle and detail to quilts. They create an opportunity to use very hot, dark, or intense color, proportionately and effectively.

Conceptually, the technique for this kind of border is two fold. First, oversize the width of the border you want to finish $^1/_8$" and the border that follows it by $^3/_8$", which gives stability while sewing. Second, trim the appropriate $^1/_4$" seam allowance to an exact $^1/_8$". This cut edge then serves as the sewing guide when adding on the next border. Success with this technique depends on accurate trimming of the $^1/_4$" seam allowance to an exact $^1/_8$" and sewing very straight, right along the cut edge of that just trimmed seam allowance.

To determine how wide to cut your border strips you must first know how wide the finished width will be. For example, imagine you want three borders. You want border one to be 1" wide finished so you would cut $1^1/_2$"-wide border strips. You want border two to finish $^1/_8$" wide so you would cut a 1" wide strip ($^1/_8$" plus $^1/_2$" usual seam allowance plus $^3/_8$" extra for stability equals 1"). You want border three (it follows the $^1/_8$" border) to finish 2" so you would cut $2^7/_8$" wide-strips (2" plus $^1/_2$" usual seam allowance plus $^3/_8$" for stability equals $2^7/_8$").

Noteworthy

The $^3/_8$" added width is adequate for stable sewing. However, this is not a magic number. It could just as well be $^1/_2$" or more. It just needs to be the same on all appropriate strips.

Specifically, the technique to create these borders follows:

1. Using the three borders as an example, sew one to two, right sides together with an accurate $^1/_4$" seam allowance. Trim this seam to an exact $^1/_8$" with the rotary cutter and ruler or mark a line and cut with scissors.
2. Press the stitches and then press the seam allowance to two.

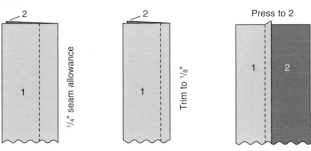

3. Place border 3 right sides together with borders 1-2 on top, with the edges of borders two and three aligned. Now sew right along the just trimmed seam allowance edge. This creates the $^1/_8$" border.
4. Trim the excess fabric to within $^1/_8$" to $^1/_4$" from the last line of stitches, press stitches, press the seam allowance to border three.

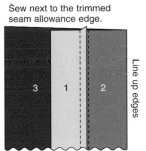
Sew next to the trimmed seam allowance edge.

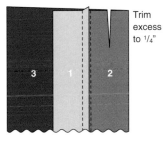 
Trim excess to $^1/_4$"

This technique is only as good as how well you trim the $^1/_4$" seam to an exact $^1/_8$" and how straight you sew next to the cut edge of the trimmed seam allowance.

Matching and Securing Points and Intersections

Successfully matching points and/or intersections requires accurate identification of seams to be matched, careful pinning, straight sewing, and well-planned pressing. After sewing, if the points or intersection are not perfectly matched, only three things could have happened. You need to improve how you identified the area, how you pinned the area, or how you sewed the area. It is very easy to remove a few stitches, realign the pieces, re-pin, and re-sew. It is not as if you only get one try. I remove stitches and re-sew as many times as it takes to successfully accomplish the task at hand. Removing stitches and re-sewing is an important part of improving the execution of the process. You don't have to be right the first time, just the last time.

The following are specific explanations of how to match several common intersections and points that we often encounter in patchwork blocks.

Simple Opposing Seams, Straight or Diagonal

You would encounter this type of intersection or matching area in a four-patch intersection for straight seams or a Card Trick block for the diagonal seams. It simply means, at the intersection or matching area, the seam allowances on one piece are pressed all to one side, and its counterpart seam allowances are pressed in the opposite direction. To match this area, align the two pieces to be sewn, right sides together, keeping edges even and together. While holding the two pieces together, separate the two pieces at the edge only and match the intersection visually and with your hands by nesting one seam allowance tightly against the other. Now close the two pieces again and secure the area with a pin placed just to the left ($1/16$") of the seam. When matching and sewing diagonal seams at a corner, begin your sewing at the corner to lock in the accuracy.

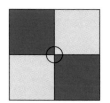

Four-Patch

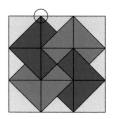

Card Trick

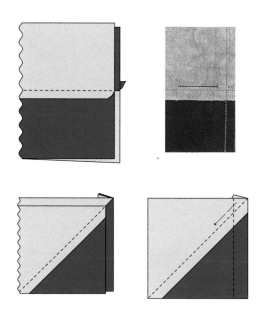

One Seam Pressed Open, One Not

To match this area, align the two pieces to be sewn, right sides together, keeping edges even and together. While still holding the two pieces together, separate them at the edge only and match the seam visually and with your hands. Position the open seam to the ridge created by the opposite seam allowances, close the pieces and secure with a pin placed just to the left ($1/16$") of the seam.

Straight or Diagonal Open Seams

To match this area, align the two pieces to be sewn, right sides together, keeping edges even and together. While still holding them together, separate them at the edge only and match the open seam lines visually and with your hands. Close the pieces and secure the area with a pin placed just to the left ($1/16$") of the seam.

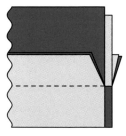

Both Seam Allowances Going in the Same Direction

There are times you must match an intersection when both seam allowances are pressed in the same direction. This seam arrangement is not ideal and places all the bulk on one side. If unavoidable, you must stabilize and match the area for sewing. While holding the two pieces right sides together, separate them at the edge only and align the seams visually and with your hands, close the area and secure with a pin placed through both the seam allowances. The

idea here is to compress and stabilize the bulk for sewing. The pin does not need to go down and then up through all the layers of fabric, which could create more distortion. Simply slide the pin through most layers, back up to the top, creating as flat a piece as possible. When sewing, seam allowances should be positioned toward the needle using the stiletto to press on the seam allowances and compress the bulk (kind of creating a groove to sew in). Sew slowly through the area, you may even need to use the hand wheel and "walk" the needle through the bulky area.

Matching Open or Opposing Straight and Diagonal Multiple Seams

Some blocks that create both open and opposing straight and diagonal seams at one intersection are Ohio Star—page 51,

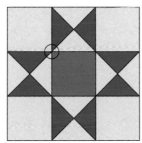

Ohio Star

Rising Star and Square—page 59, and Dutchmann's Puzzle—page 54. To match this type of intersection, hold the two pieces right sides together, keep edges even and together. While still holding the two pieces together, separate them at the edge only and match the seams visually and with your hands. Now close the two pieces and secure the intersection with a pin placed just to the left ($^{1}/_{16}$") of the seam.

Noteworthy

In my experience, I have often discovered that, when you insert the alignment pin into the point from the wrong side of the fabric, it exits out the right side incorrectly. To remedy this, when you insert the pin from the wrong side, look at how the pin exits out the right side to be sure it is at the exact point.

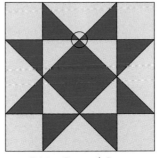
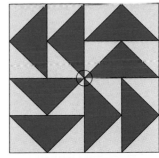

Rising Star and Square *Dutchman's Puzzle*

Alignment Pin

To match any seams or intersection that I do not have success matching visually and with my hands as described earlier, I use an alignment or positioning pin technique. This technique is always an option and could be used in any and all instances where two or more seams need to match at one point. This pin precisely aligns or matches one point or seam to another; it does not secure the area for sewing. The alignment pin is eventually removed but is necessary to match and keep the two pieces together while aligning one piece onto the other squarely and creating even edges. To match two points, place the two pieces to be sewn right sides together, and insert the alignment pin from the wrong side of one piece at the point and into the right side of the other point on the second piece, exiting through to the wrong side. Now pull the pin down straight and snug so the pin end or head rests on the fabric and is exactly matching the two points. If the pin shaft is tilted even slightly, you are skewing and shifting the points, and they will not be matched.

To secure the area for sewing, simultaneously hold the two pieces to be matched and the alignment pin straight with one hand and insert another pin just to the left and right ($^1/_{16}$") of the alignment pin. Now remove the alignment pin. If, after sewing, the points are not matched, you have pinned, sewn, or identified the area to be matched improperly and you need to correct it.

Matching Open or Opposing Diamond Seams

This type of intersection occurs in the Morning Star block, page 91, when joining and matching 45° diamond intersections. This is the one time I always use an alignment pin. To match this intersection, place the two cut segments right sides together and identify the correct edge to be sewn. Now measure down from that edge $^1/_4$" and make a mark on the seam. Turn the pair of segments over and make a mark on that seam $^1/_4$" down from the same edge. This creates a place to align and pin the intersection correctly. To match this intersection, pin through the mark and seam of one piece and into the seam and mark of the other piece. Whether the seams are open or opposing, the pin must travel through the thread area and not into any fabric. Pull the pin down, keeping edges even. Secure the area by placing a pin just to the left and right ($^1/_{16}$") of the alignment pin and then remove the alignment pin. If the intersection is not matched you either identified, pinned, or sewed improperly and you need to correct it. You must sew over the marks you make.

Matched intersection *Too much seam allowance* *Too little seam allowance*

Advantages of Sewing Individual Blocks

Because experience is always the best teacher, making individual blocks offers a variety of advantages and opportunities.

♦ The opportunity to explore and discover a variety of color and design principles by composing blocks using the Rough Cut Mock-ups and Mirrors Technique—page 23.

♦ If small piecing is new to you, I encourage you to try the 3" blocks because they offer the most opportunity for improving your sewing skills and color development. Aren't the most beautiful, valuable gifts often presented in small packages?

♦ Each block becomes a personal tutor as it offers different techniques, methods and challenges for you to experience the process without becoming connected to a large project.

♦ As you do each block, develop a reference and critique notebook. Document relevant challenges, experiences and how corrections were made.

♦ When experimenting, use solid fabrics, as they are very revealing when it comes to sewing and will show discrepancies quickly and clearly without the distraction of printed fabrics.

♦ Exploring different blocks offers variety and not monotony.

♦ Blocks offer opportunities to identify problems and learn how to correct them.

♦ Each new block you try is a clean slate.

♦ Blocks offer the opportunity to develop drafting and construction skills as they usually have an orderly, logical structure to their piecing sequence.

♦ One beautifully done block can be the beginning of a medallion style quilt.

Finally, a word of caution. The purpose of this book is to help you experiment and improve your drafting, sewing, design, and color skills. To learn how to critique and correct your own work, become a more creative quiltmaker, and to achieve quality workmanship. I urge you not to sacrifice these gifts and opportunities for fast, quick, easy sewing methods that require little, if any, sewing skills. That would defeat the purpose of this book. Foundation piecing, although accurate, only requires that you sew on a line and is much like paint-by-number. It does not offer opportunities to learn the importance of accuracy in cutting or sewing with accurate $^1/_4$" seam allowances, or proper grain line placement, or how to critique and correct your own work. All methods and techniques are valid, and have their place in quiltmaking. Choose carefully, and your choices will enhance your journey with the benefits that arise from quality workmanship.

VII The Block Collection

The Collection of Sampler Blocks

The following is a collection of forty-nine traditional style blocks. The majority are machine pieced patchwork, three are hand-appliquéd, and two are created using the English paper piecing technique. Most are representational (houses, stars, baskets, etc.) and are offered in 3", 4", and 6" sizes.

I have always loved making blocks for their orderly and logical structure. They are the basic element in quiltmaking from which most designs are developed and created. My approach to blocks has always been to make each one the very best it can be with regard to color, fabric, and workmanship; to make each block as if it were its own quilt and could stand alone.

As each block is introduced, I have suggested some noteworthy information regarding design, color, and technical considerations as well as "vital statistics" including drafting category, grid dimension (where relevant), number of shapes, number of pieces, and techniques used with page number reference. Also included is an accurate 3" pattern (with a graph line underlay so you can see how the block is drafted, where applicable) reflecting shape identifying letters, grain arrows and an actual size color photo of each block from the featured quilt. Rotary cutting information includes $^1/_4$" seam allowance and is given in three colors to distinguish the three sizes, i.e., black for 3", red for 4", and green for 6".

Noteworthy
When making the templates, you must add $^1/_4$" seam allowance to all sides of each shape, except where noted.

When templates are needed, the pattern shapes for the 3" size will be taken from the 3" pattern on each page. The 4" and 6" pattern shapes from which to make templates are with the block or on pages 118–124. The pattern size is denoted by line color, red for 4", green for 6". All 4" nine-patch drafting category blocks require templates because the dimensions of the shapes needed are not easily found on the ruler.

Fabric requirements for each block are minimal and are reflected with the cutting requirements. The blocks are presented based on their degree of difficulty and their names are what is most familiar to me although there could be, and probably are, many more. Six blocks are my own designs: Double Ohio Star—page 68, Sawtooth Double Nine-Patch—page 85, Tall Ship—page 99, Basket—page 64, Leaf Design—page 83, and Ten Pointed Star—page 97.

Before you begin each block, determine if you want to change or further fracture any areas to add more design and detail. Then determine where you will place the light, medium, and dark values before choosing color and fabric. Some blocks will offer more opportunities for color and fabric variety than others. Evaluate the block you are making and take advantage of the opportunities presented. I suggest you interview, experiment, and rearrange color and fabric choices by composing each block using the Rough Cut Mock-ups and Mirrors Technique on page 23. As you experiment, explore and make changes, always ask yourself if you are making the block better. Once you have composed your block, you are ready to cut and sew. The piecing sequence and pressing paths are given for each block.

Don't settle, let your heart sing and enjoy your journey!

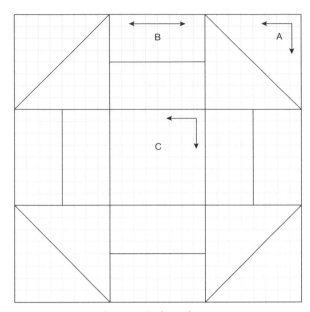

8 squares/inch graph paper

Vital Statistics

Drafting Category: Nine-patch, 6 × 6 grid
Grid Dimension: $1/2$", 1"
Number of Shapes: 3
Number of Pieces: 17
Techniques Used: Individual Half-Square Triangles—page 35, Strip Piecing—page 42, Rotary Cutting—page 26, Templates—page 27.

Noteworthy

Don't diminish the beauty of this block because of its simplicity. The large pieces are an opportunity to use larger printed fabric, especially the center square.

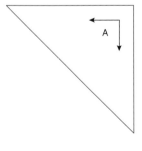

Add $1/4$" seam allowances.

Cutting

The 4" block requires templates for all shapes.
Shape A: Cut two $1^7/_8$", $2^7/_8$" squares from both background and block fabric, cut in half diagonally.
Shape B: Cut one 1" × 7", $1^1/_2$" × 12" straight grain strips from both background and block fabric. Sew strips, right sides together, down the length, open seam (3" block only) or press to dark. Develop a straight edge and cut four $1^1/_2$", $2^1/_2$" segments from the strip unit. Set aside.
Shape C: Cut one $1^1/_2$", $2^1/_2$" square from block fabric.

Piecing Sequence and Pressing Path

Arrows and circle indicate pressing direction.

Cut 4

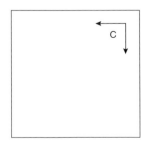

Make 4

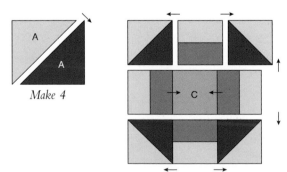

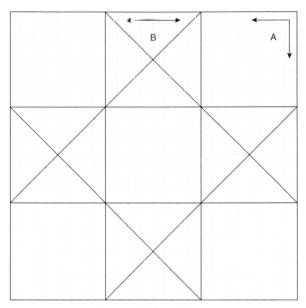

8 squares/inch graph paper

Vital Statistics

Drafting Category: Nine-patch, 6 × 6 grid
Grid Dimension: $1/2$", 1"
Number of Shapes: 2
Number of Pieces: 21
Techniques Used: Rotary Cutting—page 26, Templates—page 27, Quarter-Square Triangle Units—page 39.

Cutting

The 4" block requires templates for all shapes.
Shape A: Cut four $1^1/2$", $2^1/2$" squares from background fabric. Cut one $1^1/2$", $2^1/2$" square from block fabric.
Shape B: Cut a total of four $2^1/4$", $3^1/4$" squares and cut into quarters diagonally. One square from light fabric (background), one square from medium fabric (the four Bs that surround the center A square), two squares from dark (the star points). These value assignments are of course, only a suggestion.

Noteworthy

This is a simple block to sew; the fabric choices will make it beautiful. The cutting information will create exactly the size of shapes you need, although you always have the option to oversize and custom cut the quarter-square triangles if you prefer—page 39.

Noteworthy

Think of the positions of the four quarter-square triangles as north, south, east, west. Always keep east and west on top when sewing, always pair east with south and west with north, always press to east and west, and always sew from the 90° corner to the point. By doing this you will always keep the correct fabric in the correct position and create opposing seams.

Piecing Sequence and Pressing Path

Arrows and circle indicate pressing direction.

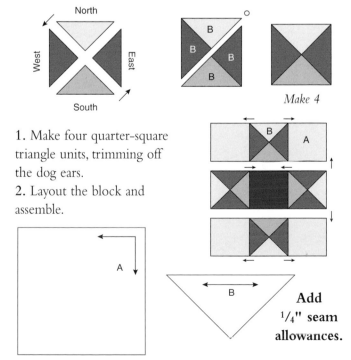

Make 4

1. Make four quarter-square triangle units, trimming off the dog ears.
2. Layout the block and assemble.

Add $1/4$" seam allowances.

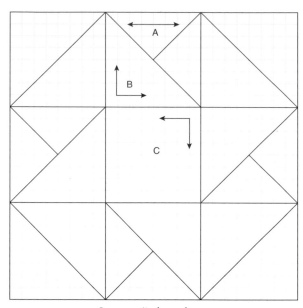

8-squares/inch graph paper

Vital Statistics

Drafting Category: Nine-patch, 6 × 6 grid
Grid Dimension: $1/2$", 1"
Number of Shapes: 3
Number of Pieces: 21
Techniques Used: Individual Half-Square Triangles—page 35, Rotary Cutting—page 26, Templates—page 27, Quarter-Square Triangle Units—page 39.

Cutting

The 4" block requires templates for all shapes.

Shape A: Cut one $2^{1}/4$", $3^{1}/4$" square of both background and block fabric, cut into quarters diagonally.

Shape B: Cut two $1^{7}/8$", $2^{7}/8$" squares of background fabric, cut in half diagonally. Cut four $1^{7}/8$", $2^{7}/8$" squares of block fabric, cut in half diagonally.

Shape C: Cut one $1^{1}/2$", $2^{1}/2$" square of block fabric.

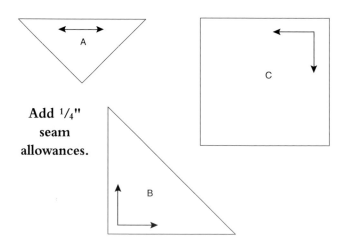

Add $1/4$" seam allowances.

Noteworthy

This block is similar in its construction to Card Trick—page 53 but has a plain square in the center position. Explore different value placements before sewing. Take care to match diagonal seams.

Piecing Sequence and Pressing Path

Arrows indicate pressing direction.

Make 4

Make 4

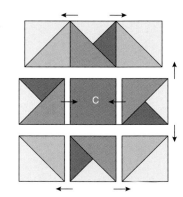

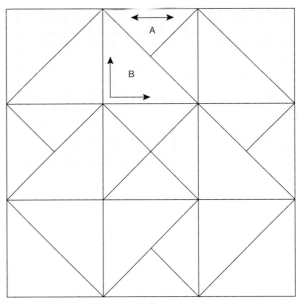

8 squares/inch graph paper

Vital Statistics

Drafting Category: Nine-patch, 6 × 6 grid

Grid Dimension: ¹/₂", 1"

Number of Shapes: 2

Number of Pieces: 24

Techniques Used: Rotary Cutting—page 26, Templates—page 27, Diagonal Seams—page 46.

Cutting

The 4" block requires templates for all shapes.

Shape A: Cut one 2¹/₄", 3¹/₄" square of background. Cut one 2¹/₄", 3¹/₄" square from each Card Trick fabric. Cut all squares into quarters diagonally. You will have two waste triangles for each trick fabric.

Shape B: Cut two 1⁷/₈", 2⁷/₈" squares of background fabric. Cut one 1⁷/₈", 2⁷/₈" squares of each Card Trick fabric, cut all squares in half diagonally.

Noteworthy

Evaluate value placement carefully before sewing. You must be able to see the four tricks. You could use four different values of one color, four different colors, or use two colors twice. Take care to match diagonal seams.

Piecing Sequence and Pressing Path

Arrows indicate pressing direction.

1. Lay out all pieces of block.

2. Sew four BB Units, four AAB Units and one AAAA Unit as shown.

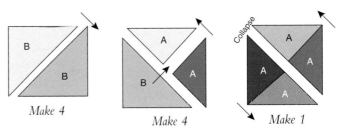

Make 4

Make 4

Make 1

3. Layout block again and assemble units into rows, and rows into the completed block.

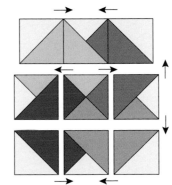

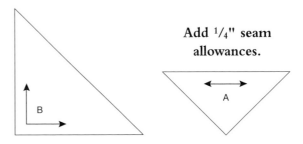

Add ¹/₄" seam allowances.

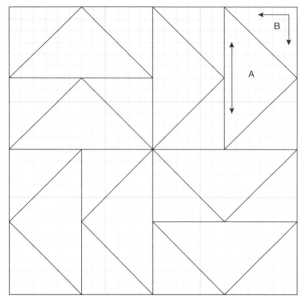

8 squares/inch graph paper

Vital Statistics

Drafting Category: Four-patch, 4 × 4 grid
Grid Dimension: $3/4$", 1", $1^1/_2$"
Number of Shapes: 2
Number of Pieces: 24
Techniques Used: Rotary Cutting—page 26, Double Half-Square Triangle Units—page 40.

Noteworthy

This block could have multiple "looks" depending on value placement. Experiment and do some mock-ups and interviewing. It is an easy block to sew but does have eight seams intersecting in the center, match it well.

Cutting

Shape A: Cut eight $1^1/_4$" × 2", $1^1/_2$" × $2^1/_2$", 2" × $3^1/_2$" rectangles from block fabric.
Shape B: Cut sixteen $1^1/_4$", $1^1/_2$", 2" squares from background fabric.

Piecing Sequence and Pressing Path

Arrows and circle indicate pressing direction.

1. Create eight ABB Units, referring to Double Half-Square Triangle Units Technique on page 40 and diagram at right.

Make 8

2. Join two ABB Units four times, join two pairs of ABB Units twice.

3. Join complete block.

Make 4

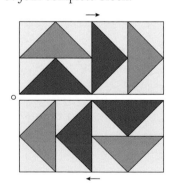

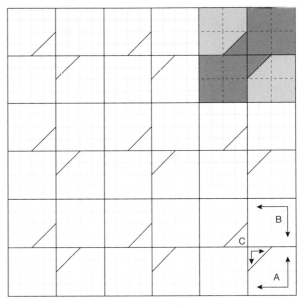

8 squares/inch graph paper

Vital Statistics

Drafting Category: Four-patch, 4 × 4 grid
Grid Dimension: $1/4$" grid makes a 1" bow tie. A $1/2$" grid makes a 2" Bow Tie.
Number of Shapes: 3
Number of Pieces: 6
Techniques Used: Rotary Cutting—page 26, Sew and Flip—page 41.

Cutting

The following information makes one bow tie. The first number makes a 1" tie, the second number makes a 2" tie.
Shape A: Cut two 1", $1^1/2$" squares of background fabric.
Shape B: Cut two 1", $1^1/2$" squares of tie fabric.
Shape C: Cut two $3/4$", 1" squares of tie fabric.

Piecing Sequence and Pressing Path

Arrows indicate pressing direction.

1. Draw a diagonal line on the wrong side of both C squares.

2. Referring to the Sew and Flip method on page 41, sew a C square onto each A background square.

Make 2

3. Lay out AC squares with B squares. Sew two pairs together; join the two pairs to create the tie block. Repeat steps 1 through 3 to make as many bow ties as you need.

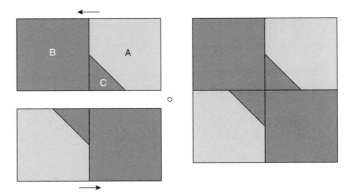

Noteworthy

A 3" block holds nine 1" ties, a 4" block can hold four 2" ties or sixteen 1" ties, a 6" block can hold nine 2" ties or thirty-six 1" ties. Use one background fabric throughout and a different tie fabric for each bow tie. Think about each tie as if it were going to be worn, and use checks, stripes, paisleys, plaids.

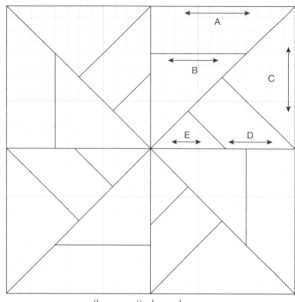

8 squares/inch graph paper

Vital Statistics

Drafting Category: Four-patch, 2 × 2 grid
Grid Dimension: 1½", 2", 3" for single pinwheel in one block
Grid Dimension: ¾", 1" for four pinwheels in one block
Number of Shapes: 5
Number of Pieces: 20
Techniques Used: Rotary Cutting—page 26, Strip Piecing—page 42, Templates—page 27.

Cutting

All strips, both straight and bias grain, are cut generously wide, except the D shape strip which is cut exactly the width needed, including seam allowances. Make one triangle template that includes both AB and CDE. Transfer both the CDE and AB lines from the pattern to the template. The lines will correspond to the seams of each strip unit for proper placement. The following will make one individual pinwheel.

Template right side up

Shape A: Cut one straight grain strip 1" × 6", 1" × 10",1½" × 10", 1½" × 12", 2" × 16" from background fabric.
Shape B: Cut one straight grain strip 1¼" × 6", 1½" × 10", 2" × 10", 2¼" × 12", 3" × 16" from block fabric.
Shape C: Cut one bias strip 1¼" × 6", 1¾" × 10", 2" × 10", 2¼" × 12", 3" × 16" from background fabric.
Shape D: Cut one bias strip ¾" × 6", ¾" × 10", 1" × 10", 1⅛" × 12", 1½" × 16" from block fabric.
Shape E: Cut one bias strip 1" × 6", 1¼" × 10", 1½" × 10", 1½" × 12", 2" × 16" from block fabric.

Noteworthy

The pinwheel is created using both straight grain and bias grain strip units. Four fabrics are used, including the background. The E shape requires a strong intense color to show up against the D and B shapes. The pinwheel is constructed in four quadrants and then those are joined to complete the block. You have the option of making a single pinwheel (3", 4" or 6") or making multiple pinwheels within one 3", 4" or 6" block. Both are used in the featured quilt. A 3" block holds four 1½" pinwheels, a 4" block holds four 2" pinwheels, and a 6" block holds four 3" pinwheels.

Piecing Sequence and Pressing Path

Arrows and circle indicate pressing direction.

AB Units

1. Sew the straight grain A and B strips together, press to B or block fabric, trim.
2. Place the template face down on the wrong side of the strip unit, the dashed line on the seam line. Trace four times and cut out.

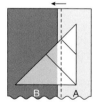

Template face down
Cut 4

CDE Units

1. Sew the bias grain CD and E strips together, handle carefully, press both seams away from the D strip, trim.
2. Place the triangle template face down on the wrong side of the strip unit, E strip should be on the left. Match lines

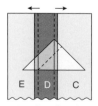

Template face down
Cut 4

on the template to the seam lines; trace around the template four times, cut out, removing the drawn lines. If both lines on the template do not exactly match both seams on the strip unit, match longest line to DC seam consistently. The AB triangle and the CDE triangle should be the same size.

Assembly

1. Lay out all eight triangles to form the pinwheel. Join one AB Unit to a CDE Unit, press to AB Unit and trim. Each ABCDE quadrant should measure $1^1/4$", $1^1/2$", 2", $2^1/2$", $3^1/2$".

2. Sew two ABCDE quadrants together twice. Press seams in opposite directions.

3. Sew the two pairs together to complete the pinwheel, open or collapse the seam, page 33.

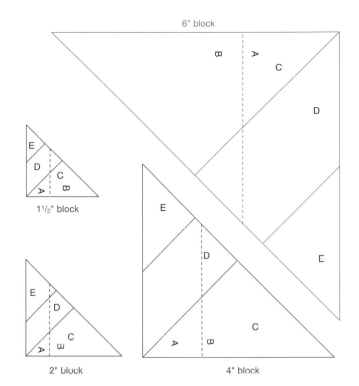

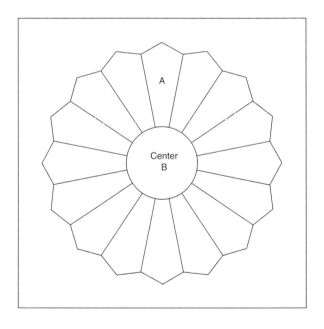

Vital Statistics

Drafting Category: Miscellaneous (sixteen equal divisions of a circle, each being 22.5°)

Grid Dimension: Use the template for all sizes to monitor sewing

Number of Shapes: 2

Number of Pieces: 17

Techniques Used: Hand Appliqué—page 44, Templates—page 27.

Cutting

Template A includes seam allowances, Shape B does not.

Shape A: Cut sixteen from plate fabrics.

Shape B: Center circle fabric will be chosen and cut later. The background square (4", 5", 7") can be cut later once the plate is assembled, so you can place it on different backgrounds to determine the best choice.

Piecing Sequence and Pressing Path

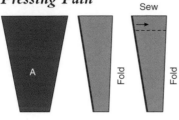

1. Fold the shape A in half, lengthwise, right sides together; align edges exactly and finger press well. Sew across the wide end, from raw edges to fold, with a small stitch length.

2. Trim the seam allowance to a generous $1/8$" and turn right side out, carefully using a toothpick or similar tool to extend the point. Manipulate the shape so it is symmetrical, and press. It is helpful to work from the back of the shape to determine symmetry. The seam allowance will lie to one side or the other, just be consistent. Repeat these instructions fifteen times.

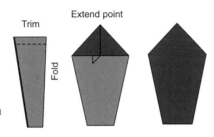

3. Lay out the sixteen plate shapes in the order you choose, in a circle. You will assemble the plate by first

Noteworthy

There are numerous approaches to color/fabric for this block. You could use sixteen different fabrics, or two fabrics repeated eight times, or four fabrics repeated four times, or eight fabrics repeated twice. Try to stay balanced in both color and value. A rough-cut mock-up is suggested.

joining pairs together, then joining two pairs, then joining two foursomes, etc.

4. Align two shape A's on top of one another accurately and sew from C to D. Keep edges together, repeat for two more shapes. Do not press or trim seam allowances until the plate is complete.

   Note: To eliminate thread tails at C edge, begin sewing two stitches in from point C, backstitch to edge, continue forward.

5. Sew two pairs together to get one quarter of the circle, aligning shapes and seams. Place template A over the two inside shapes to check for accuracy and symmetry. Create three more quarters.

6. Sew two quarters together twice, aligning shapes and seams.

7. Sew the two halves together, aligning and sewing as described earlier.

8. Evaluate carefully, press all seams in one direction and trim seams.

9. Trace shape B onto freezer paper and cut out exactly. Refer to Appliqué—page 44, for further instruction. Appliqué to the center of the plate, using a matching thread.

10. Turn plate over, trim to expose paper, leave a $1/8$" seam allowance, lift fabric edge from paper edge with a toothpick. Remove paper circle carefully with tweezers.

11. Lay the plate on different backgrounds to interview. Cut a 4", 5", 7" square of chosen background fabric, fold into quarters horizontally and vertically as well as diagonally and press.

12. Center the plate onto the background square and appliqué in place, matching thread. You may have to use several different threads.

13. Trim the background square to $3^1/2$", $4^1/2$", $6^1/2$".

14. Place the block face down on a soft surface and steam from the back.

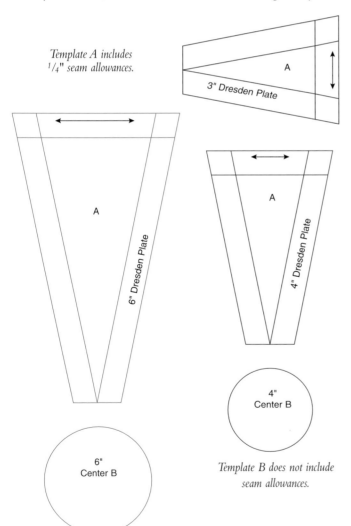

Template A includes $1/4$" seam allowances.

A

3" Dresden Plate

A

6" Dresden Plate

A

4" Dresden Plate

6" Center B

4" Center B

Template B does not include seam allowances.

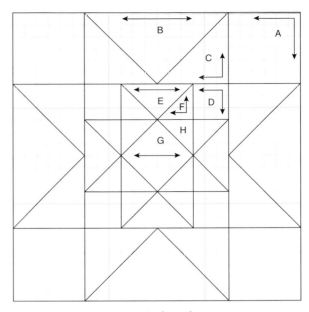

8 squares/inch graph paper

Vital Statistics

Drafting Category: Four-patch 8 × 8 grid
Grid Dimension: Outer Star $^3/_4$", 1", $1^1/_2$", Inner Star $^3/_8$", $^1/_2$", $^3/_4$"
Number of Shapes: 7
Number of Pieces: 37
Techniques Used: Rotary Cutting—page 26, Double Half-Square Triangle Units—page 40, Sew and Flip—page 41.

Cutting

You will be cutting only rectangles and squares, no triangles.
Shape A: Cut four $1^1/_4$", $1^1/_2$", 2" squares from background fabric.
Shape B: Cut four $1^1/_4$" × 2", $1^1/_2$" × $2^1/_2$", 2" × $3^1/_2$" rectangles from background fabric.
Shape C: Cut eight $1^1/_4$", $1^1/_2$", 2" squares from star point fabric.
Shape D: Cut four $^7/_8$", 1", $1^1/_4$" squares from background fabric.
Shape E: Cut four $^7/_8$" × $1^1/_4$", 1" × $1^1/_2$", $1^1/_4$" × 2" rectangles from background fabric.
Shape F: Cut eight $^7/_8$", 1", $1^1/_4$" squares from star point fabric.
Shape G: Cut one $1^1/_4$", $1^1/_2$", 2" square from center fabric.
Shape H: Cut four $^7/_8$", 1", $1^1/_4$" squares from star point fabric.

Piecing Sequence and Pressing Path

Arrows and circles indicate pressing direction.

1. Referring to Double Half-Square Triangle Units technique—page 40, make four BCC Units for the large outer star and four EFF Units for the small star.

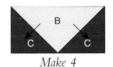

Make 4

Make 4

2. Referring to the Sew and Flip technique—page 41, make one GHHHH unit.
3. Lay out the small star and assemble.
4. Lay out the complete block and assemble.

Make 1

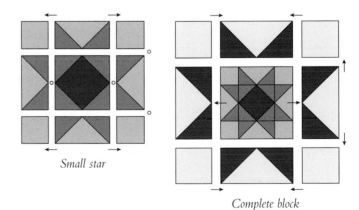

Small star

Complete block

Noteworthy

Explore value placement with this block; there are many options. Create high contrast when doing the small star between the background and star points.

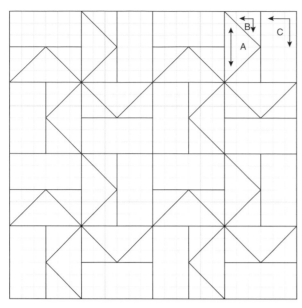

8 squares/inch graph paper

Vital Statistics

Drafting Category: Four-patch, 8 × 8 grid
Grid Dimension: $3/8$", $1/2$", $3/4$".
Number of Shapes: 3
Number of Pieces: 16
Techniques Used: Rotary Cutting—page 26,
Double Half-Square Triangle Units—page 40.

Cutting

The following information is for making a single pinwheel.
Shape A: Cut four $7/8$" × $1^1/4$", 1" × $1^1/2$", $1^1/4$" × 2"
rectangles of block fabric.
Shape B: Cut four $7/8$", 1", $1^1/4$" squares of block fabric and
background fabric.
Shape C: Cut four $7/8$" x $1^1/4$", 1" × $1^1/2$", $1^1/4$" × 2"
rectangles of background fabric.

Piecing Sequence and Pressing Path

Arrows and circles indicate pressing direction.

1. From the A rectangles and B squares (both block and background fabrics) make four double half-square triangle units—page 40. The block fabric B should be applied to the right side of the A rectangle as you look at it right side up.

Make 4

2. Join a background rectangle to each of the four ABB Units. Each ABBC Unit should measure $1^1/4$", $1^1/2$", 2" square.

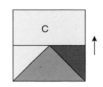

Make 4

3. Lay out the four ABBC Units, assemble and press. Four complete pinwheels are needed to make one whole block.

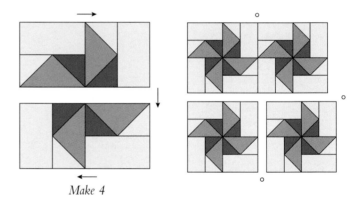

Make 4

Noteworthy

Four small pinwheels ($1^1/2$", 2", 3") make up a whole 3", 4", or 6" block. This block is created by using only rectangles and squares. You will make four quadrants and then join those to complete the pinwheel. Using a deep dark or bright for the inside B triangles and creating high contrast between the background and the larger A triangle makes the pinwheel easy to read. This is a great block set on point.

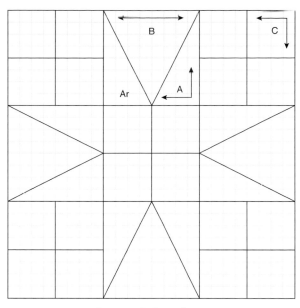

8 squares/inch graph paper

Vital Statistics

Drafting Category: Nine-patch, 6 × 6 grid
Grid Dimension: $1/2$", 1"
Number of Shapes: 3
Number of Pieces: 32
Techniques Used: Rotary Cutting—page 26, Templates—page 27.

Noteworthy

This is a simple block created with two units, a star point unit and a four-patch unit. Determine value placement carefully so you can see both.

Cutting

Make templates for Shape A and B for the 3" and 6" block. Make templates for all shapes for the 4" block.

Shape A and Ar: Cut four each from star point fabric.
Shape B: Cut four from background fabric.
Shape C: Cut eight 1", $1^1/_2$" squares from background fabric, cut twelve 1", $1^1/_2$" squares from block fabric.

Noteworthy

Cutting and sewing individual squares for the four patches rather than sewing strips offers more opportunity for variety of color and fabric.

Piecing Sequence and Pressing Path

Star point units and four patch units should all measure $1^1/_2$", $2^1/_2$" square. Use templates to monitor 4" block units.

1. Sew Ar to B, matching dots but sewing edge to edge. Add A to B, similarly, repeat three times.
2. Sew four C's together, repeat four times.

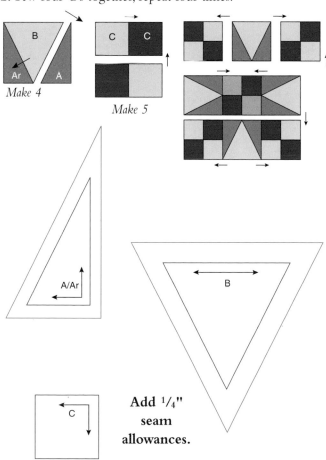

Make 4

Make 5

Add $1/4$" seam allowances.

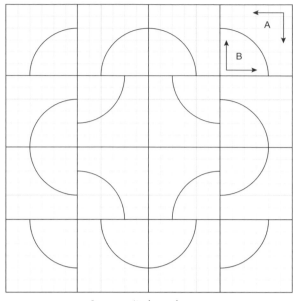

8 squares/inch graph paper

Vital Statistics

Drafting Category: Four-patch, 4 × 4 grid
Grid Dimension: $3/4$", 1", $1^1/2$"
Number of Shapes: 2
Number of Pieces: 32
Techniques Used: Rotary Cutting—page 26,
Templates—page 27.

Cutting

Make a template for shape B for all block sizes, adding $1/4$"
seam allowance to the straight sides only, not the curve.

Shape A: Cut sixteen $1^1/4$", $1^1/2$", 2"
squares of background fabric.

Shape B: Trace template onto dull side of
freezer paper sixteen times and cut out.
Press freezer paper shapes onto wrong side
of desired fabric, shiny side down, leaving a
little space between each one. Apply glue
tube to both paper and fabric, about $3/16$"
from curved edge only; let dry. Cut out
shapes, leaving a $3/16$" seam allowance from
curved edge; bring fabric over curved edge
of paper.

Apply Glu-tube adhesive

Bring fabric over paper edge.

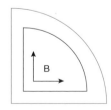

Add $1/4$" seam allowances to straight sides only.

Piecing Sequence and Pressing Path

Arrows indicate pressing direction.

Make 16

1. Place B shape onto A square,
matching corner and straight edges,
hot tape in place.
2. Appliqué shape B's curved edge
to A square 16 times, matching thread
to shape B.
3. Remove paper carefully so as not to distress stitching.
4. Cut away the A square corner under Shape B to within
$3/16$" of appliqué stitches for
the 6" block only. Leave all
fabric in place for the 3"
and 4" blocks.
5. Lay out all AB Units
appropriately.
6. Join units into rows, and
rows into the completed
block.

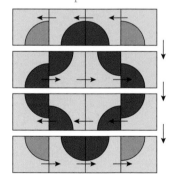

Noteworthy

The two shapes, A concave and B convex, create
numerous designs in addition to this one. Feel free to
explore other options. The joining of A's and B's into
squares is done by appliqué. The squares are then
arranged appropriately and joined together into rows
and then into the completed block.

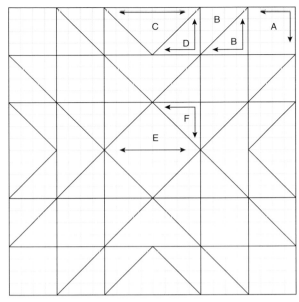

8-squares/inch graph paper

Vital Statistics

Drafting Category: Nine-patch, 6 × 6 grid
Grid Dimension: $1/2$", 1"
Number of Shapes: 4
Number of Pieces: 53
Techniques Used: Stitched Grid—page 36, Templates—page 27, Double Half-Square Triangle Units—page 40, Sew and Flip—page 41, Rotary Cutting—page 26, Oversize and Custom Cut—page 36.

Cutting

The 4" block requires templates for Shapes A, C and E only because the Shape A square template is used to custom cut the BB Units and to cut the D and F shapes that begin as squares.

Shape A: Cut four 1", $1^1/2$" squares from both background and block fabrics.

Shape B: Eight pairs of B's will be made using the Stitched Grid method (oversized) for all block sizes. Cut one $3^1/2$", 4", $4^1/2$" squares of both background and block fabrics.

Shape C: Cut four 1" × $1^1/2$", $1^1/2$" x $2^1/2$" rectangles from both background and block fabrics.

Shape D: Cut sixteen 1", $1^1/2$" squares of block fabric, draw a diagonal line on the wrong side of each one.

Shape E: Cut one $1^1/2$", $2^1/2$" square of block fabric.

Shape F: Cut four 1", $1^1/2$" squares of block fabric, draw a diagonal line on each one.

Noteworthy

Evaluate block carefully and decide value placement before cutting.

Piecing Sequence and Pressing Path

Arrows and circles indicate pressing direction.

1. Make four of Unit one. Make eight pairs of B's referring to the Stitched Grid method—page 36. Custom cut a 1", $1^1/2$" square from the eight oversized half-square triangles. If making the 4" block, use template A to custom cut the BB Unit. 4" patterns—page 120. Join two BB Units to two Shape A squares four times.

2. Make four of Unit 2. Refer to Double Half-Square Triangle Units—page 40 and make eight. Join two together four times to make four Unit 2's.

3. Make one Unit 3. Using the Sew and Flip method—page 41, add the four F squares to the larger E square.

4. Lay out the block and assemble the units into the rows and join the rows to complete the block.

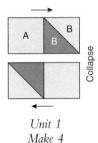

Unit 1
Make 4

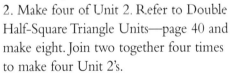

Unit 2
Make 4

Unit 3
Make 1

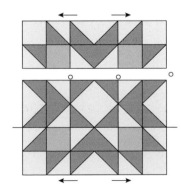

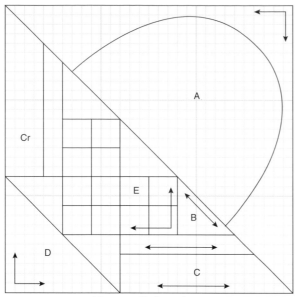

10 squares/inch graph paper

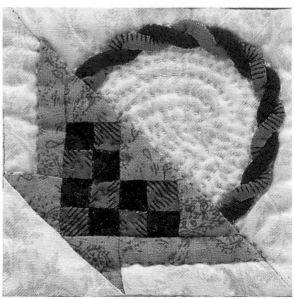

Block design by Sally Collins

Vital Statistics

Drafting Category: Five-patch

Grid Dimension: Use templates for all sizes to monitor sewing.

Number of Shapes: 7 including handle

Number of Pieces: 25 including handle

Techniques Used: Rotary Cutting—page 26, Templates—page 27, Metal Bias Bar—page 42, Strip Piecing—page 42, Oversize and Custom Cut—page 36.

Cutting

Make accurate templates for all shapes (A, B, C, D, E). Shape E is the large square made up of four smaller squares. Shape C and Cr is the large shape made from both basket and background fabric. Transfer appropriate reference lines on templates A, C, and E. Patterns are on page 118.

Shape A: Cut one from background fabric.

Shape B: Cut five from a basket fabric.

Shape C and Cr: Cut one strip of both background and basket fabric 1" × 6", 1" × 6", $1\frac{1}{2}$" × 10".

Shape D: Cut one from background fabric.

Shape E: Cut one strip from two chosen fabrics 1" × 8", $1\frac{1}{4}$" × 10", $1\frac{1}{2}$" × 10".

Handle: Cut one $\frac{7}{8}$" × 12" bias strip from two different fabrics.

Piecing Sequence and Pressing Path

Arrows and circle indicate pressing direction.

The C and Cr Unit and the E units are made by using the oversize and custom cut techniques.

1. Make one C and one Cr Unit. Sew the appropriate background and basket fabric strips together down the length, press towards the basket fabric. Place the C template face

down on the wrong side of the strip unit, matching thread line to the line on the template; trace, dot and cut out. Turn template over (face up) and trace, dot and cut out.

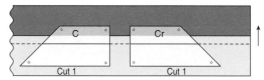

2. Make three E Units. Pair and sew the E strips together down the length, press to dark (or open for 3" block), trim. Cut six 1", 1", $1\frac{1}{2}$" segments off the strip unit. Sew two segments to create a four-patch, matching center intersection and outside edges, press. Place E template face down on the wrong side of the oversized four-patch, trace and cut. Repeat for the remaining four segments.

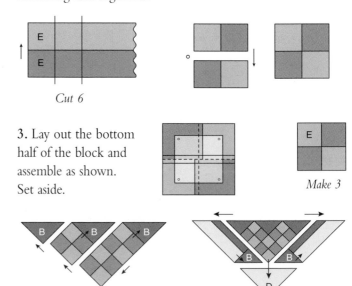

3. Lay out the bottom half of the block and assemble as shown. Set aside.

4. Make the handle for all sizes using the ⅛" bias bar. Refer to Metal Bias Bar, page 42, for further instructions.

5. Transfer the handle shape to the background A shape. The placement line indicates the outer edge of the handle. Following the diagram, use Roxanne's Glue-Baste-It and weave the two bias pieces directly to the background. It is much easier than you might think.

6. Lay out both halves of the basket block. Join at the center seam, press. Hand appliqué edges of the handle bias in place.

Noteworthy

There are many exposed bias edges as you piece this block so take care with the iron. Be sure the two handle fabrics show up against one another and the background. Use your fabrics cleverly, stripes work great cut on the bias for the handle.

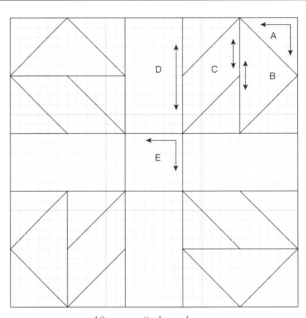

10 squares/inch graph paper

Jack-in-the-Box

Vital Statistics

Drafting Category: Five-patch, 5 × 5 grid
Grid Dimension: Use templates for all sizes to monitor sewing.
Number of Shapes: 5
Number of Pieces: 29
Techniques Used: Templates—page 27, Double Half-Square Triangle Units—page 40.

Cutting

Make only two templates, Shape E square and Shape D rectangle.
Shape E: Cut sixteen from background fabric, draw a diagonal line on the wrong side of all these squares; they will become Shape A. Cut one Shape E from block fabric for the center.

Shape D: Cut four from each medium block fabric; these will become Shape B. Cut four from each dark block fabric; these will become Shape C. Cut four from a block fabric; these are the rectangles that separate the four corner sub-blocks and connect to the center E square.

Noteworthy

Although there are five different shapes that make up this block, you will construct it using only the E square and the D rectangle and the Double Half-Square Triangle Units technique. One approach to this block is to create the illusion of depth by choosing four different colors, a dark and medium of each. Make each shape C the dark and each shape B the medium.

Piecing Sequence and Pressing Path

Arrows indicate pressing direction.

1. This block is created from two different units, four AAB and four AAC. Construct both units using the Double Half-Square Triangle Units technique—page 40, but change the direction of the diagonal.

2. Lay out all the units appropriately. Join an AAB to an AAC four times.

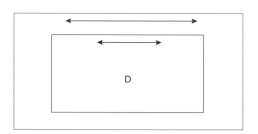

Add ¹/₄" seam allowances.

3. Lay out the four joined units with the four remaining D rectangles and the center E square. Assemble and press.

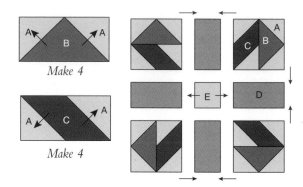

Make 4

Make 4

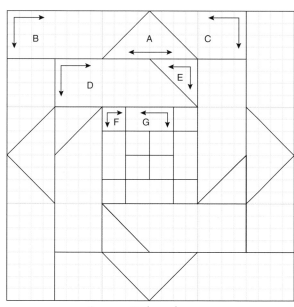

8 squares/inch graph paper

Interlocking Squares

Vital Statistics

Drafting Category: Nine-patch, 6 × 6 grid
Grid Dimension: ¹/₂", 1"
Number of Shapes: 7
Number of Pieces: 32
Techniques Used: Rotary Cutting—page 26, Templates page—27, Partial Seaming—page 43, 67.

Cutting

The 4" block requires templates for all shapes. Patterns are on page 119.

Shape A: Cut one 2¹/₄", 3¹/₄" square of block fabric, cut into quarters diagonally.

Shape B and C: Cut one 1" × 42", 1¹/₂" × 42" strip of background fabric, cut in half.

Shape D: Cut four 1" × 2", 1¹/₂" × 3¹/₂" rectangles of block fabric.

Shape E: Cut four 1", 1¹/₂" squares of block fabric.

Shape F: Cut eight ³/₄", 1" squares of block fabric.

Shape G: Cut four ³/₄" × 1", 1¹/₂" × 1" rectangles of block fabric.

Piecing Sequence and Pressing Path

Arrows indicate pressing direction.

This block is assembled by first making three different units: four ABC Units, four DE Units and one FG Unit. Once the units are made, lay out your block and assemble the units into the completed block using the partial seaming technique that will be described.

1. Make four ABC Units.

a. Cut a 45° angle on one end of both the B and C background strips as shown.

b. Cut tips off the A triangle by measuring from the center out $3/4$", $1^1/4$" in both directions.

c. Sew A to B, press to B. You will be sewing two bias edges together, handle them very carefully.

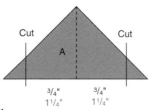

d. Sew C to the AB Unit, press to C. Repeat (a) through (d) three times. Check to be sure the top of the A triangle is a 90° angle when the unit is complete.

e. On each ABC Unit measure from the center of A out to the right $1^1/4$", $2^1/4$" and draw a line with a removable marking tool. Now measure from the center of Shape A out to the left $1^3/4$", $3^1/4$" and draw a line. It should measure from line to line 3" × 1", $5^1/2$" × $1^1/2$". If correct, cut on the drawn lines.

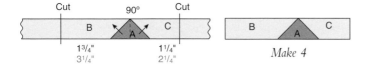

Make 4

2. Make four DE Units.

a. Draw a diagonal line on the wrong side of Shape E.

b. Place E square onto D rectangle as shown and sew just on the scrap side of the line. Bring the E corner to meet the D corner, press to E and trim. Repeat three times. Unit should measure 2" × 1", $3^1/2$" × $1^1/2$".

Make 4

3. Make one FG Unit.

a. Sew four F's together as shown, open seams for the 3" block.

b. Sew four F's to two G's as shown.

 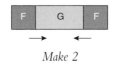

Make 1

Make 2

c. Lay out the F's and G's as shown and join the three rows into the completed FG Unit. Unit should measure $1^1/2$", $2^1/2$" square.

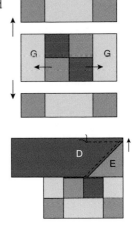

4. To complete the block requires the partial seaming technique. This simply means you will sew the first seam part way instead of edge to edge and complete the partial seam after all other pieces needed for that section are added. No backstitching is needed.

a. Partially sew a DE Unit to the FG Unit as shown.

b. Add three DE Units clockwise as shown.

c. Complete the partial seam. Unit should measure $2^1/2$", $4^1/2$" square.

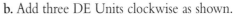

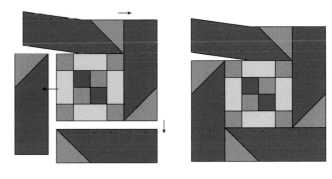

5. Add four ABC Units to the DEFG Unit, using the partial seaming technique described above, to complete the block.

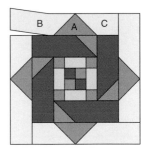

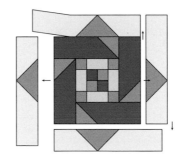

Noteworthy

Take care to maintain a 90° angle when sewing Shape A into place. If the angle is off, the block will look and be tilted. Interview and choose your fabrics carefully, being sure there is adequate value change in the interlock area for the image to be successful.

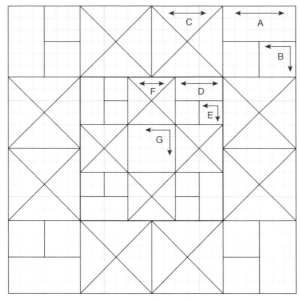

8 squares/inch graph paper

Block design by Sally Collins

Vital Statistics

Drafting Category: Inner Star is a nine-patch, 6 × 6 grid, Outer Star is a four-patch, 8 × 8 grid.

Grid Dimension: Inner Star $1/4$", $1/2$", Outer Star $3/8$", $1/2$", $3/4$"

Number of Shapes: 7

Number Pieces: 73

Techniques Used: Oversize and Custom Cut—page 36, Rotary Cutting—page 26, Quarter-Square Triangle Units—page 39, Templates—page 27.

Cutting

Shape A: Cut one strip $1^1/4$" × 10", 1" × 10", $1^1/4$" × 10" of background fabric, sub-cut into four $1^1/4$" × 2", 1" × $1^1/2$", $1^1/4$" × 2" rectangles.

Shape B: Cut four $1^1/4$", 1", $1^1/4$" squares from both background and block fabrics.

Shape C: Cut eight $2^1/2$", $2^1/4$", $2^3/4$" squares, two from background and six from block fabric, cut all into quarters diagonally.

Shape D: Cut one $1^1/8$" × 10", 1" × 7" strip from background fabric; sub-cut into four $1^1/8$" × $1^3/4$", 1" × $1^1/2$" rectangles.

Shape E: Cut four $1^1/8$", 1" squares from both background and block fabric.

Shape F: Cut four $2^1/4$", $2^1/4$" squares, one from background and three from block fabric, cut all into quarters diagonally.

Shape G: Cut one 1", $1^1/2$" square from block fabric.

Note: The inner star shapes D, E, F and G for the 4" size require templates.

Piecing Sequence and Pressing Path

Arrows and circles indicate pressing direction.

1. Make four DEE Units.
2. Make four ABB Units.

Note: For the 3" block only, custom cut the DEE Units into a 1" square, custom cut the ABB units into a $1^1/4$" square.

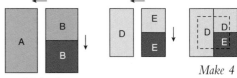

Make 4

Make 4

3. Make four F Units.
4. Make eight C Units.

Note: For the 3" block only, custom cut the F Units into a 1" square, custom cut the C Units into a $1^1/4$" square.

Make 8

Make 4

Noteworthy

This block has lots of pieces and opportunities for subtle but effective color changes. One way to relate or connect the inner star to the outer star would be through repetition of color and/or fabric placement in the corner squares of both stars. The oversize technique applies to all shapes for the 3" block only, except for Shape G. The 4" and 6" blocks are cut and sewn actual size. Take care to match diagonal seams.

5. Layout the block. You must sew the inner star first and then continue to sew the block together.

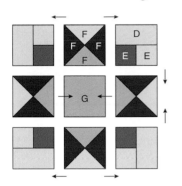

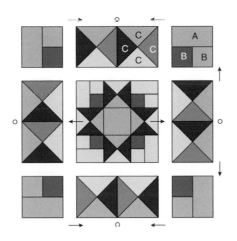

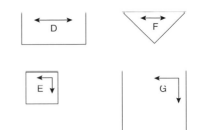

Add ¹/₄" seam allowances.

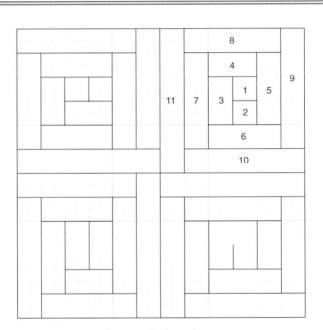

8 squares/inch graph paper

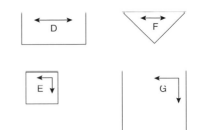

Log Cabin

Vital Statistics

Drafting Category: Nine-patch, 6 × 6 grid
Grid Dimension: ¹/₄", ¹/₂"
Number of Shapes: 6
Number of Pieces: 11
Techniques Used: Rotary Cutting—page 26, Templates — page 27, How to Measure—page 22.

Noteworthy

For this block use five light fabrics and six dark. You must focus on sewing straight to maintain the grid and create straight seam lines. Four small blocks make up the complete block.

Cutting

The 4" block requires templates for Shapes 1/2, 3/4, 5/6, 7/8, 9/10, and 11. All but Shape 11 are used twice in each of the four small blocks. Patterns are on page 119.

Cut one ³/₄" × 9", 1" × 18" straight grain strip of five light and six dark fabrics. Obviously the length of the strips you need increases as the block grows. The length of the cut strips is generous.

Piecing Sequence and Pressing Path

Arrows and circle indicate pressing direction.
1. Arrange the strips in numerical order.
2. Sew Fabric 1 and 2 together lengthwise, right sides together, with an accurate ¹/₄" seam allowance. To help keep the edges aligned, it is helpful to press the two strips together before sewing.

3. Press the stitches, then press seam toward Fabric 2 and trim. This two-strip unit should measure 1", $1\frac{1}{2}$" across.

4. Cut four $\frac{3}{4}$", 1" segments from the two-strip unit, using lines on the ruler to help line up with the seam lines. The success of this block depends on the squareness of the center, so be sure to cut and then sew very straight and accurately.

Note: I suggest you cut at least eight segments so that when you have completed the sewing you can choose the four best small blocks to make the larger block. It won't take you any longer to sew eight blocks than it will four.

5. Place Fabric 3 (dark) right side up, close to your sewing machine needle, and

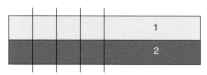

place a 1-2 segment right side down onto the Fabric 3 strip. Position the segment so that the seam allowance is toward you and the edges are matched. Sew very slowly and straight, with an accurate $\frac{1}{4}$" seam allowance, using a stiletto or similar tool to help guide the pieces. Sew completely off the end of the segment before placing the next one down for sewing. Continue until all the segments have been sewn onto the strip.

6. Press the stitches and cut the segments apart, lining up the ruler lines with the seam lines. Trim seams and press to Fabric 3. These units should now measure 1", $1\frac{1}{2}$" square.

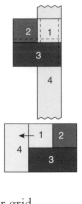

7. Place Fabric 4 (light) right side up, close to your sewing machine needle. Place the 1-2-3 segment right side down, onto Fabric 4, positioned so that the last strip added on is closest to you and the seam allowance is toward you. This positioning is necessary throughout the block. Sew with an accurate $\frac{1}{4}$" seam allowance.

8. Continue cutting, pressing, and sewing segments in the same manner as described above. Add strips in numerical order. Be aware of your grid dimension and measure the segments after adding each strip. One completed small block should measure 2", $2\frac{1}{2}$", $3\frac{1}{2}$".

9. Layout the four blocks and arrange them to your liking.

10. Assemble as shown.

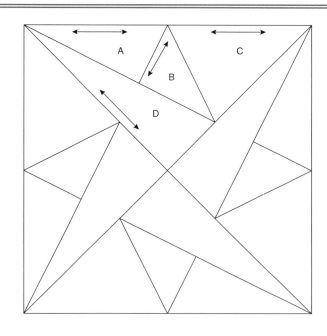

Vital Statistics

Drafting Category: Miscellaneous

Grid Dimension: Use templates for all sizes to monitor sewing.

Number of Shapes: 4

Number of Pieces: 16

Techniques Used: Templates—page 27.

Cutting

Shape A: Cut four from background fabric.
Shape B: Cut four from block fabric.
Shape C: Cut four from background fabric.
Shape D: Cut four from block fabric.

Piecing Sequence and Pressing Path

Arrows and circles indicate pressing direction.

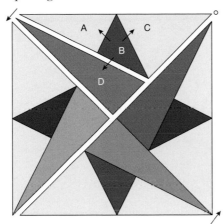

You will pin at dots for proper alignment of fabric shapes, but always sew from edge to edge. You will first create four ABCD Units, then join two units to create two halves, then join the two halves to complete the block.

Noteworthy

If you look at this block as two stars, one with long points on top of one with shorter points, you could choose two fabrics or colors, one for each. If you see D and its corresponding B as one continuous shape (in an over/under fashion), you could choose two values (one dark, one medium) of four different colors and arrange them so that D was medium and its corresponding B would be the dark. Or choose just two colors, each with a dark and medium value, and use each twice. This block uses templates to assemble and will have numerous exposed bias edges so handle carefully. Take advantage of having templates to use your fabric cleverly.

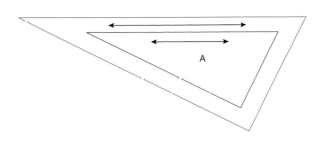

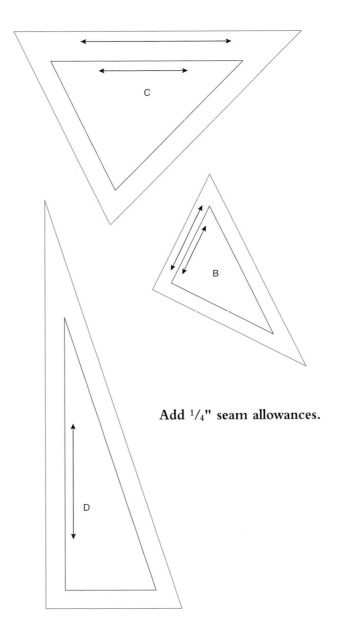

Add ¹/₄" seam allowances.

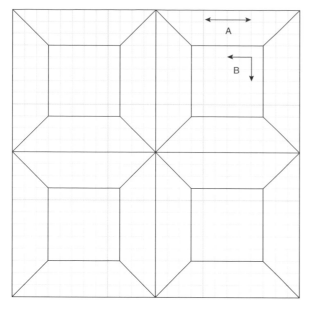

8 squares/inch graph paper

Vital Statistics

Drafting Category: Four-patch, 8 × 8 grid
Grid Dimension: $^3/_8$", $^1/_2$", $^3/_4$"
Number of Shapes: 2
Number of Pieces: 20
Techniques Used: Y-Seam Construction—page 41, Templates—page 27, Diagonal Seams—page 46.

Cutting

All block sizes require templates.
Shape A: Cut eight each from background and block (spool) fabrics.
Shape B: Cut four from block fabric (thread).

Noteworthy

Use your fabrics cleverly to create the spools. Stripes are an obvious, effective choice for the thread area, and could all be different (Shape B). The Shape A spool ends could be the same color/fabric.

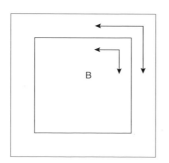

Piecing Sequence and Pressing Path

Arrows and circles indicate pressing direction.
1. Sew two background A's to B square. Sew from dot to dot, backstitching at both dots.
2. Sew two spool Fabric A's to the same B square, sewing again from dot to dot and backstitching.
3. Sew corners from outside edge to dot and backstitch.
4. Each individual spool should measure 2", $2^1/_2$", $3^1/_2$". Repeat steps 1-3 three more times.
5. Assemble complete block.

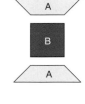

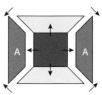

Make 4

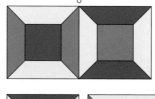

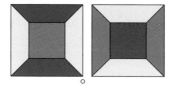

Add $^1/_4$" seam allowances.

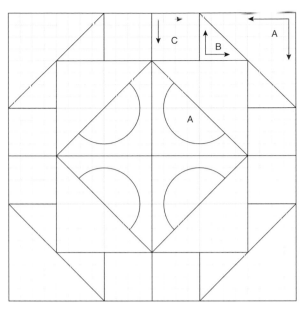

8 squares /inch graph paper

Vital Statistics

Drafting Category: Nine-patch, 6 × 6 grid
Grid Dimension: $1/2$", 1"
Number of Shapes: 3 plus handle
Number of Pieces: 28 plus four handles
Techniques Used: Rotary Cutting—page 26, Templates—page 27, Metal Bias Bars—page 42.

Cutting

The 4" block requires templates for all shapes. Patterns are on page 119.

Shape A: Cut four $1^7/_8$", $2^7/_8$" squares from background and cut in half diagonally. Cut one $1^7/_8$", $2^7/_8$" square from each basket fabric, cut in half diagonally. This will yield two triangles from each fabric; you only need one.

Shape B: Cut one $1^3/_8$", $1^7/_8$" square from each basket fabric, cut in half diagonally.

Shape C: Cut eight 1", $1^1/_2$" squares from background.

Basket Handles: Cut one $^7/_8$" × 4", $^7/_8$" × 6", 1" × 8" bias strip from each basket fabric.

Noteworthy

All sizes of the block will need a template for Shape A, reflecting the handle placement line on it so you can transfer that to your fabric. The 3" and 4" basket will use the $^1/_8$" bias bar for the handle and the 6" basket will use the $^1/_4$" bias bar for its handle.

Piecing Sequence and Pressing Path

Arrows and circles indicate pressing direction.

Handles

1. Mark the basket handle placement line on the four background Shape A triangles. See page 119 for 4" and 6" handle placement. Refer to Metal Bias Bars, page 42, for further instructions.

2. Glue-baste the four handles in place, positioning the raw edges of the handle seam allowance toward the line. The line indicates the outside edge of the handle. Do not appliqué edges until block is complete.

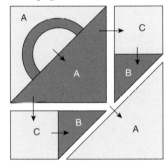

Make 4

Basket

1. Assemble basket as shown. Repeat for the remaining three baskets.

2. Sew the four baskets together to complete the block and appliqué the handle edges in place.

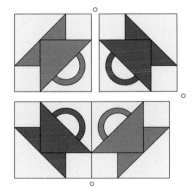

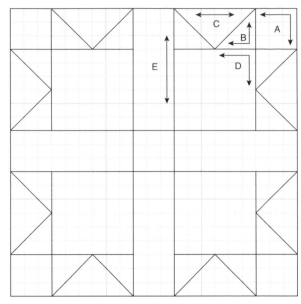

7 squares/inch graph paper

Vital Statistics

Drafting Category: Seven-patch

Grid Dimension: Use templates for all sizes to monitor sewing.

Number of Shapes: 5

Number of Pieces: 37

Techniques Used: Templates—page 27, Mock-Ups/Mirrors—page 23.

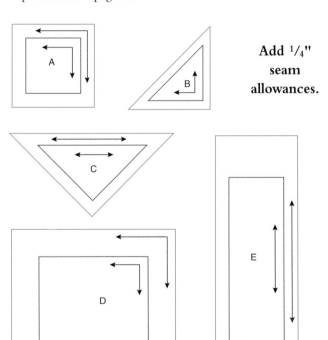

Add ¼" seam allowances.

Cutting

Shape A: Cut one for the center from block fabric, cut four from background fabric.

Shape B: Cut sixteen from block fabric.

Shape C: Cut eight from background fabric.

Shape D: Cut four from block fabric.

Shape E: Cut four from background fabric.

Piecing Sequence and Pressing Path

Arrows indicate pressing direction.

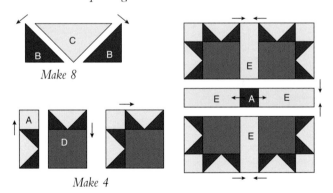

Make 8

Make 4

Noteworthy

Take advantage of having templates. The D shape is the largest and an opportunity to custom cut something beautiful from a larger multi-colored printed fabric or border print. Make a mock-up of one quarter of the block and use the mirrors to interview fabrics before actually cutting out the whole block.

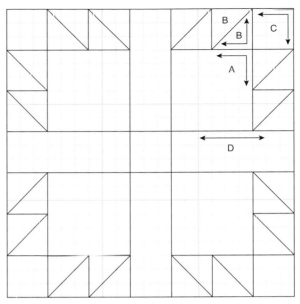

7 squares/inch graph paper

Vital Statistics

Drafting Category: Seven-patch, 7 × 7 grid
Grid Dimension: Use templates for all sizes to monitor sewing.
Number of Shapes: 4
Number of Pieces: 45
Techniques Used: Templates—page 27, Stitched Grid—page 36, Oversize and Custom Cut—page 36, Mirrors—page 23.

Cutting

Make templates for Shapes A, C, and D only for all block sizes. Patterns are on page 119. The BB Units will be created using the Stitched Grid Half-Square Triangle method (oversized)—page 36, and then custom cut from those units with the C-shape template. The square C-shape template should reflect the BB diagonal line to properly place it on the oversized unit for accurate custom cutting of the BB Unit.

Shape A: Cut four from block fabric.
Shape B: 16 pairs of B's will be made using the Stitched Grid Method—page 36. Cut two 3½", 3¾", 4¼" squares from both background and toe fabric. You will create the stitched grid twice, each will yield eight pairs of B's from which you will use the Shape C template to custom cut.

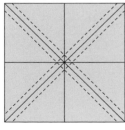

Make 2

Shape C: Cut four from background fabric, cut one from block fabric.
Shape D: Cut four from background fabric.

Piecing Sequence and Pressing Path

Arrows indicate pressing direction.

Make 4

Make 4

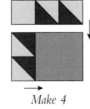
Make 4

1. Layout all the shapes and BB Units. Be sure triangles are positioned correctly.
2. Sew eight pairs of BB Units together as shown; four pairs positioned in one direction and four pairs positioned in the other direction.
3. Lay out the block again. Following the diagram, create four paws.
4. Assemble the complete block.

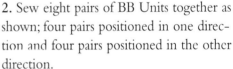
Make 2

Make 1

Noteworthy

You can interview your fabric choices by composing one quarter of the block (or one paw) and then use the mirrors to "see" the whole block. You might find a multi-colored busier print or a great plaid for the A shape and use a quieter, darker fabric of one or more of the colors in the multi-colored busier print or plaid for the toes.

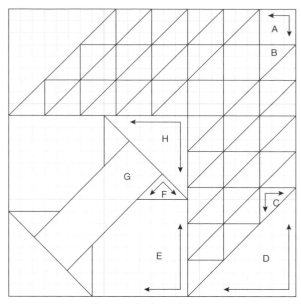

8 squares/inch graph paper

Vital Statistics

Drafting Category: Four-patch, 8 × 8 grid,
Grid Dimension: $3/8$", $1/2$", $3/4$"
Number of Shapes: 8
Number of Pieces: 68
Techniques Used: Rotary Cutting—page 26, Individual Half-Square Triangles—page 35, Square-to-Square—page 38, Oversize and Custom Cut—page 36, Mock-Ups/Mirrors—page 23, Sticky Note—page 38, Templates—page 27.

Cutting

All block sizes require a template for Shape E only.

Shape A: Cut three $7/8$", 1", $1^1/4$" squares of background fabric.

★Shape B: Cut twenty-four $1^1/4$", $1^1/2$", $1^3/4$" squares of both background and tree fabric.

Shape C: Cut three $1^1/4$", $1^3/8$", $1^5/8$" squares of tree fabric, cut in half diagonally.

Shape D: Cut one 2", $2^3/8$", $3^1/8$" square of background, cut in half diagonally.

Shape E: Cut two from background fabric.

Shape F: Cut two $1^1/4$", $1^3/8$", $1^5/8$" squares of trunk fabric, cut in half diagonally.

Shape G: Cut one 1" × $1^7/8$", $1^1/16$" x $2^7/16$", $1^1/4$" × $3^1/2$" strip of trunk fabric.

Shape H: Cut one $1^3/4$", 2", $2^1/2$" square of background fabric, cut in half diagonally.

★Square-to-Square and Oversize and Custom Cut Technique is used to create the twenty-four BB half-square triangle units because it requires less preparation time, so you can pursue a variety of fabric and color. An open-toed sewing machine foot is helpful when using this technique.

Piecing Sequence and Pressing Path

Arrow and circle indicate pressing direction.

1. Pair a background B square and tree fabric B square right sides together and sew diagonally from corner to corner. Because the B squares are oversized, you can use the sticky note technique for sewing diagonally, which eliminates the need to mark a line. Press stitches, trim to $1/4$" seam allowance. Open seam and trim again to a generous $1/8$".

2. Custom cut a $7/8$", 1", $1^1/4$" square from this oversized unit. Repeat twenty-three times.

3. Layout out entire block and assemble it in three different units: Unit 1 (should measure $1^5/8$" × $2^3/8$", 2" × 3", $2^3/4$" × $4^1/4$"), Unit 2 (should measure $1^5/8$" × $3^1/2$", 2" × $4^1/2$", $2^3/4$" × $6^1/2$"), and the Trunk Unit (should measure $2^3/8$", 3", $4^1/4$" square).

4. Join Unit 1 to Trunk Unit, press to Unit 1.

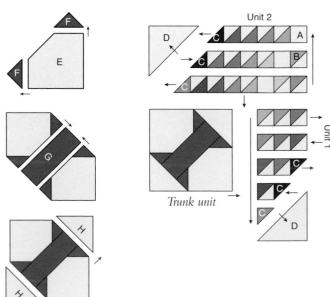

5. Add Unit 2 to Unit 1/Trunk Unit, press to Unit 1/Trunk.

If the 6" Pine Tree block seems empty you could add additional leaves, Shape I. Refer to the Tree project on page 114 to see how it looks. Here is how to make one additional leaf.

1. Cut two $1\frac{1}{4}$" squares of background fabric, cut in half diagonally, one triangle will be waste.

2. Cut one $1\frac{1}{4}$" square of leaf fabric, cut in half diagonally, one will be waste.

Noteworthy

The half-square triangles must be divided equally at the corners, and you must join them together with a very straight seam to insure that all points remain complete. One approach to color would be to mock-up fifteen different colors/fabrics on a background creating half the tree and placing a mirror appropriately to interview your choices and "see" the whole tree—page 24.

3. Lay out the four triangles and join as shown.

4. You will eliminate a BB half-square triangle for each leaf you add and replace it with a $1\frac{5}{8}$" leaf fabric square, cut in half diagonally, same as Shape C; one will be waste. Join the large leaf and small leaf as shown.

Extra leaf option

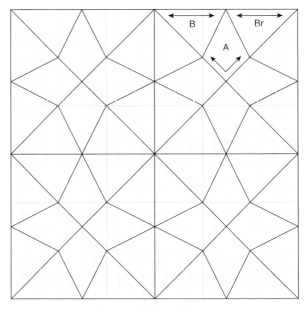

Add $\frac{1}{4}$" seam allowances.

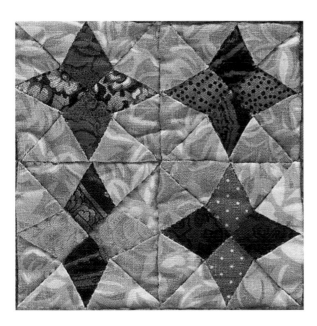

Vital Statistics

Drafting Category: Nine-patch, 3 × 3 grid
Grid Dimension: Use templates for all sizes to monitor sewing.
Number of Shapes: 2
Number of Pieces: 12
Techniques Used: Templates—page 27.

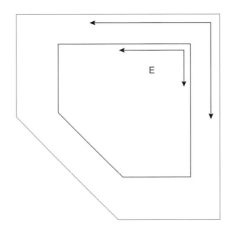

8 squares/inch graph paper

Noteworthy

Four small stars ($1\frac{1}{2}$", 2", 3") make up a whole 3", 4" or 6" block. Although templates are used to create this block, all sewing is done from edge to edge. To create more interest in the block you could split the A shape vertically, transfer that line to your template and place it on a strip unit comprised of two different fabrics, and then cut out the shape as described in the Five-Pointed Star block—page 98.

Cutting

The following information makes one small block; you need four for a whole block.

Shape A: Cut four from block fabric.

Shape B and Br: Cut four each from background fabric.

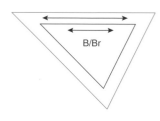

Add ¼" seam allowances.

Piecing Sequence and Pressing Path

Arrows and circle indicate pressing direction.

You will create four quadrants or ABBr Units and then join them together to create the whole block. Handle exposed bias edges carefully.

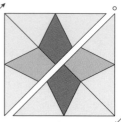

Make 4

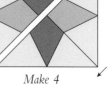

Make 4

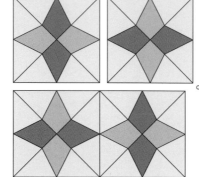

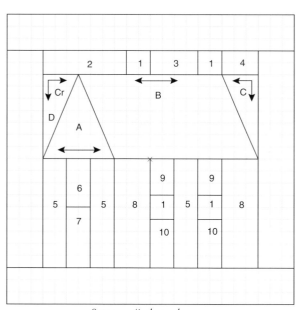

8 squares/inch graph paper

Vital Statistics

Drafting Category: N/A

Grid Dimension: N/A

Number of Shapes: 13

Number of Pieces: 22

Techniques Used: Rotary Cutting—page 26, Templates—page 27.

Cutting

You will need templates for Shapes A, B, C, and D. Patterns are on page 120. If you are making the 3" house the C and D shapes are exactly the same, so you can make only the C shape and turn it over (reverse) to create D.

Shape 1: Cut two ³/₄", ⁷/₈", 1¹/₈" squares from chimney fabric, cut two from window fabric.

Shape 2: Cut one 1³/₈" × ³/₄", 1³/₄" × ⁷/₈", 2¹/₂" × 1¹/₈" rectangle from sky fabric.

Shape 3: Cut one 1" × ³/₄", 1¹/₄" × ⁷/₈", 1⁷/₈" × 1¹/₈" rectangle from sky fabric.

Shape 4: Cut one ⁷/₈" × ³/₄", 1" × ⁷/₈" rectangle, 1¹/₈" square from sky fabric.

Shape 5: Cut three 1⁵/₈" × ³/₄", 2¹/₈" × ⁷/₈", 3¹/₈" × 1¹/₈" rectangles, two from house front fabric and one from house side fabric.

House

Shape 6: Cut once 1" × ³/₄", 1¹/₄" × ⁷/₈", 1⁵/₈" × 1¹/₈" rectangle from house front fabric.

Shape 7: Cut one ³/₄" × 1¹/₈", 1³/₈" × ⁷/₈", 2" × 1¹/₈" rectangle of door fabric.

Shape 8: Cut two 1⁵/₈" × ⁷/₈", 2¹/₈" × 1", 3¹/₈" × 1¹/₄" rectangles from house side fabric.

Shape 9: Cut two ⁷/₈" × ³/₄", 1" × ⁷/₈", 1¹/₄" × 1¹/₈" rectangles from house side fabric.

Shape 10: Cut two 1" × ³/₄", 1¹/₄" × ⁷/₈", 1³/₄" × 1¹/₈" rectangles from house side fabric.

Shape A: Cut one from roof fabric.
Shape B: Cut one from roof fabric.
Shape C: Cut one from sky fabric.
Shape D: Cut one from sky fabric. (If making the 3" size, you can reverse C template for this shape).

Piecing Sequence and Pressing Path

Arrows indicate pressing direction.

X identifies the center of all block sizes. You will sew the house together in rows, i.e., chimney row, roof row, and house side/front row.

1. Lay out all the pieces appropriately.

2. Sew the three rows together. Each row should measure 2³/₄", 3³/₄", 5³/₄" long.

3. Join the three rows, matching outside edges and appropriate intersections. The house should now measure 2³/₄", 3³/₄", 5³/₄" square.

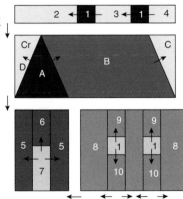

4. Add sashing strips onto the sides, top and bottom of the house to bring it up to 3¹/₂", 4¹/₂", or 6¹/₂" square. Fabric could be anything you choose. Perhaps sky fabric for the two sides and the top and a grass fabric for the bottom.

5. Cut two ⁷/₈" × 2³/₄", ⁷/₈" × 3³/₄", ⁷/₈" × 5³/₄" strips of fabric and sew to the two sides of the house, press to sashing strip. House should now measure 3¹/₂" × 2³/₄", 4¹/₂" × 3³/₄", 6¹/₂" × 5³/₄".

6. Cut two ⁷/₈" × 3¹/₂", ⁷/₈" × 4¹/₂", ⁷/₈" × 6¹/₂" strips of fabric and sew to the top and bottom of the house. House should now measure 3¹/₂", 4¹/₂", 6¹/₂" square.

Note: If your house does not measure what it should before adding the sashing strips, cut strips wider than ⁷/₈" and then trim equally from all sides to bring your house to 3¹/₂", 4¹/₂", 6¹/₂". The center X will aid you in trimming. From the center, measure out one half of the final measurement for your house in all directions (1³/₄", 2¹/₄", 3¹/₄").

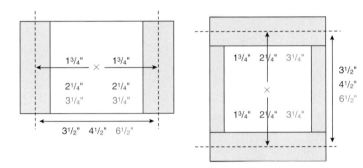

Noteworthy

The house image alone does not measure 3", 4", or 6". You will add fabric strips to all four edges of the house to bring it to the appropriate size. There are four design areas to this block, the chimney/sky area, the roof area, the house front area under the roof, Shape A and the house side area under the roof Shape B. I usually choose two values (medium and dark) of two different colors for the house. One color is for the two roof shapes and one color for the house side/front. The placement of values depends on where you have the light source coming from. For example, let's say my two colors are black for the roof area and purple for the house side/front. If I choose for the light to come from the side of the house, then Shape B would be

medium black and the house side would be medium purple. The roof, Shape A would be dark black and the house front would be the dark purple. It is most important to sew straight when making this block, and I suggest not using a directional or check fabric for the house front or side, as I did. There are so many pieces and seams it is a very choppy area, and unless you are carefully matching the print of the fabric it can look distracting. There are a lot of numbers in the cutting instructions so choose your block size and focus only on that color or number. To help you keep your place when reading the cutting information, use the edge of another piece of paper to underline the relevant line you are reading.

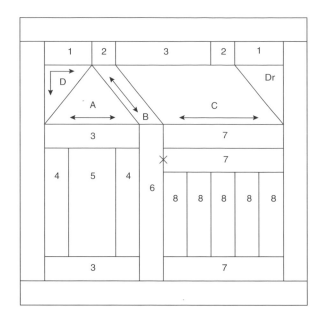

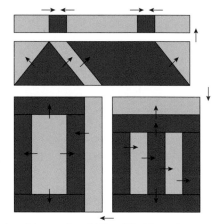

Vital Statistics

Drafting Category: Miscellaneous
Grid Dimension: $1/8$" or multiples of, $1/4$" or multiples of
Number of Shapes: 12
Number of Pieces: 24
Techniques used: Rotary Cutting—page 26, Templates—page 27.

Cutting

The 4" block requires templates for all shapes.

Shape 1: Cut two $3/4$" × 1", 1" × $1^1/2$" rectangles from background fabric.

Shape 2: Cut two $3/4$", 1" squares from house fabric.

Shape 3: Cut one $3/4$" × $1^1/2$", 1" × $2^1/2$" rectangle of background fabric, cut two from house fabric.

Shape 4: Cut two $3/4$" × $1^5/8$", 1" × $2^3/4$" rectangles from house fabric.

Shape 5: Cut one 1" × $1^5/8$", $1^1/2$" × $2^3/4$" rectangles from background fabric.

Shape 6: Cut one $3/4$" × $2^1/8$", 1" × $3^3/4$" rectangle from background fabric.

Shape 7: Cut two $3/4$" × $1^3/4$", 1" × 3" rectangles from house fabric, cut one from background fabric.

Shape 8: Cut three $3/4$" × $1^3/8$", 1" × $2^1/4$" rectangles from house fabric, cut two rectangles from background fabric.

Noteworthy

The house image itself is not the block size. Background sashing strips are added to bring it to the appropriate size. This is a very traditional design, usually done in two colors/fabrics, background and house fabric.

Shape A: Cut one from house fabric.
Shape B: Cut one from background fabric.
Shape C: Cut one from house fabric.
Shape D and Dr: Cut one each from background fabric.

Piecing Sequence and Pressing Path

Arrows indicate pressing direction.

1. Sew schoolhouse together in three rows: chimney row, roof row and side/front row.

2. Join rows to complete the schoolhouse. Schoolhouse should measure 3", $5^1/2$" square.

3. Cut two background sashing strips $3/4$" × 3", 1" × $5^1/2$" and add to the two sides of the schoolhouse.

4. Cut two strips of background fabric $3/4$" × $3^1/2$", 1" × $6^1/2$" and add to the top and bottom of the schoolhouse.

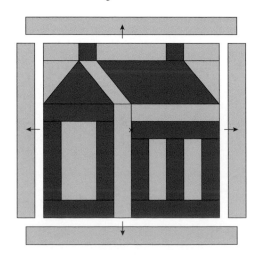

Noteworthy

If your schoolhouse does not measure accurately, you will cut your background sashing strips generously wider and longer than instructed and trim using the center "X". Use a ruler to find the center of your 4" or 6" block. See House page 78–79 for details on trimming. If you are making the 4" schoolhouse, cut all your background sashing strips 1" wide by the length of your house and trim. Add top and bottom background sashing strip similarly. The idea here is once the schoolhouse image is created, the added background sashing strips bring the house up to either 3½", 4½", or 6½" square.

Add ¼" seam allowances.

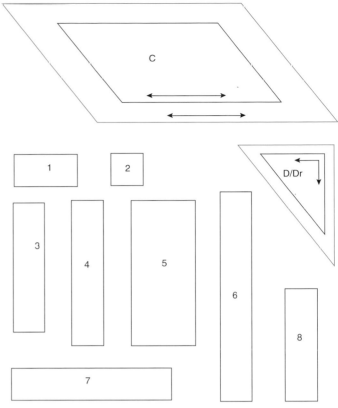

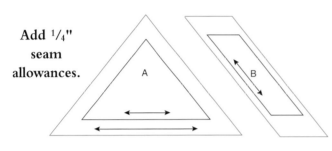

Vital Statistics

Drafting Category: 60° diamonds
Number of Shapes: 1

Noteworthy

Notice that the center is identified by the "x", not where the six seams intersect. You will need a light, medium, and dark of three different colors to create a traditional look and the illusion of dimension.

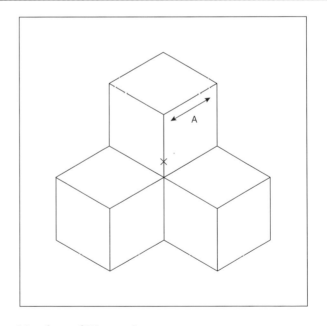

Number of Pieces: 9
Techniques Used: English Paper Piecing—page 43.

Preparation

4" and 6" patterns are on page 119.

Trace and cut out nine diamond shapes from the block pattern onto the dull side of freezer paper. Be sure all the diamond shapes are exactly the same to maintain equality of shapes and ensure they will sew together well. Refer to the English Paper Piecing on page 43 for further instructions.

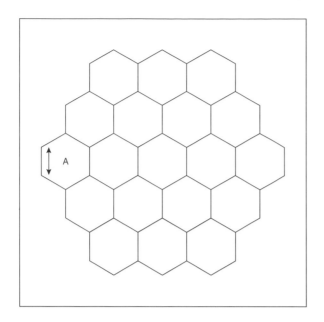

Vital Statistics

Drafting Category: Hexagons
Number of Shapes: 1
Number of Pieces: 19
Techniques Used: English Paper Piecing—page 43.

Preparation

Trace and cut out nineteen hexagon shapes from freezer paper, refer to English Paper Piecing on page 43 for further instructions.

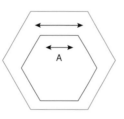

Noteworthy

This block is traditionally done with a yellow center, then the six surrounding hexagons create the flower, and the twelve surrounding hexagons become the leaves. With regard to value, the center is often the lightest, the flower area a medium and the leaves a dark. This is only a suggestion, use your imagination.

Vital Statistics

Drafting Category: Appliqué
Number of Shapes: 4 including stem

Number of Pieces: 22
Techniques Used: Hand Appliqué—page 44, Metal Bias Bars—page 42, Mock-ups/Mirrors—page 23.

Preparation

Leaf and Heart Shapes: Trace and cut out six Shape 2 leaves, fourteen Shape 3 leaves and one Heart on the dull side of freezer paper. Refer to Hand Appliqué—page 44 for further instructions.

Stem: Use the 1/8" bar for the 3" and 4" block, the 1/4" bar for the 6" block. Cut one bias strip from stem fabric 7/8" × 10", 7/8" × 10", 1" × 13"; refer to Metal Bias Bars—page 42 for further instructions.

Noteworthy

When I made the 3" block, I reduced the number of leaves to sixteen. Experiment and change anything you like. Use the basting glue sparingly. Be sure to wait until block is complete to remove paper from the back. Also note that there are two different sizes of leaves within the design. To help decide color/fabric you could mock-up one half of the design and use your mirrors.

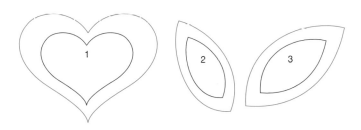

Leaf Design

Block design by Sally Collins, see Medallion Sampler.

Vital Statistics

Number of Shapes: 2
Number of Pieces: 20–22
Techniques Used: Appliqué—page 44, Mirrors—page 23.

Preparation

Trace twenty shape A leaves and one each of shapes B and C center circles on the dull side of freezer paper. Refer to Appliqué—page 44, for further information. 4" and 6" patterns are on page 124.

Noteworthy

When planning your color and fabric you could think of the design as all leaves and do gradation of green or you could think of the center eight shapes as flower petals, the next row of eight could be leaves and the final corner shapes as flower buds. Make a mock-up of one quarter of the design and use the mirrors. Refer to *My Journey*—page 104, row 2, block 2, which shows how the design could be rearranged and expanded when placed in the 6" host block.

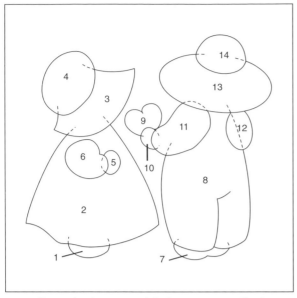

Pattern has been reversed for freezer paper appliqué

Vital Statistics

Number of Shapes and Pieces: 14
Techniques Used: Hand Appliqué—page 44.

Preparation

Trace each shape onto the dull side of the freezer paper. Refer to Hand Appliqué—page 44 for further instructions. 6" pattern on page 121.

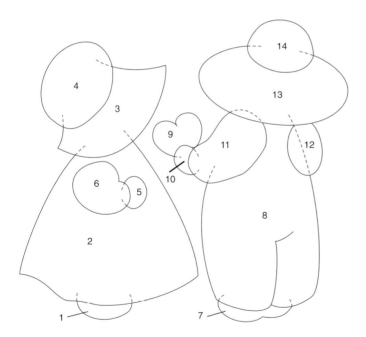

Noteworthy

When I saw this block I thought it was the cutest thing I'd ever seen. Angie Woolman of Oakland, California shared it in one of my classes and has given me permission to share it with you, although the origin of the design is unknown. Remove the paper as you appliqué if there is an open edge. Remove the paper from the back for enclosed shapes. You can assemble Bill and Sue offsite and then applique them onto the background or appliqué the individual shapes onto the background in numerical order. Whatever method you use, make clear placement markings onto your background. I embroidered around the edge of the heart to more clearly define it. You could personalize this block by changing the heart to something else like a balloon or flower, etc. Choose clothes fabrics carefully, especially for the small blocks, keeping edges of shapes highly defined from one another.

Block design by Sally Collins

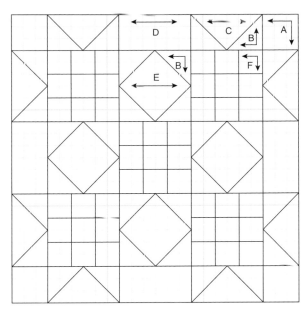

8 squares/inch graph paper

Vital Statistics

Drafting Category: Star points four-patch 8 × 8 grid, nine-patch, 3 × 3 grid

Grid Dimension: Star points four-patch $3/8$", $1/2$", $3/4$", nine-patch $1/4$", $1/2$"

Number of Shapes: 6

Number of Pieces: 97

Techniques Used: Rotary Cutting—page 26, Double Half-Square Triangle Units—page 40, Strip Piecing—page 42, Sew and Flip—page 41, Templates—page 27.

Noteworthy

Although this is a relatively simple block to sew, it has a lot of pieces so be vigilant to measuring and maintaining the appropriate grid dimension. An open-toed sewing machine foot is helpful when using the Double Half-Square Triangle Units technique. When evaluating your work, notice if you are creating equality among the shapes, especially the nine-patch squares. There are numerous opportunities for color and fabric. I found it helpful to choose either the star points or the nine patches to be most prominent in the block visually. Then place the darkest fabric in that position. Do a lot of interviewing (mock-up) before cutting and sewing. Have plenty of value and texture changes even if the number of colors is only one or two.

Cutting

Shape A: Cut four $7/8$", 1", $1 1/4$" squares from background fabric.

Shape B: Cut thirty-two $7/8$", 1", $1 1/4$" squares of star point fabric.

Shape C & D: Cut one $7/8$" × 18", 1" × 24", $1 1/4$" × 40" strip of background fabric and sub-cut into twelve $7/8$" × $1 1/4$", 1" × $1 1/2$", $1 1/4$" × 2" rectangles.

Shape E: Cut four $1 1/4$", $1 1/2$", 2" squares from background.

Shape F: Nine-patches: for each different color or fabric combination cut three length-grain strips $3/4$" × 6", 1" × 6" from a dark and from a medium to medium light fabric. This cutting is generous for one nine-patch. The 4" block requires a template for Shape F.

Piecing Sequence and Pressing Path

This block consists of three units, two different Star Point Units (BCB and EBBBB) and a nine-patch Unit (F). Make the units first, then lay out the block with the other background pieces. *Arrows indicate pressing direction.*

1. Make eight Star Point Units BCB, refer to Double Half-Square Triangle Units technique, page 40. Make four Star Point Units EBBBB, refer to Sew-and-Flip technique, page 41.

Make 8

Make 4

Note: For the 3" and 4" blocks, trim out the B triangle only, leave the C rectangle or E square in place.

2. Make five nine-patches: sew a dark/medium/dark strip unit and a medium/dark/medium strip unit. Carefully press seams after each strip is added, press both seams in the same direction. Strip units should measure 1¼", 2" wide. For each nine-patch cut two ¾", 1" segments from the dark/medium/dark unit and cut one ¾", 1" segment from the medium/dark/medium strip unit.

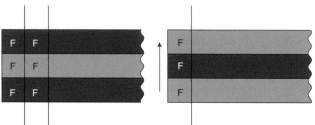

Arrange as shown, turning segments to create opposing seams from row to row. Join rows, pressing seams in one direction. A nine-patch unit should measure 1¼", 1½", 2" square. If you are making the 3" block, you will need to trim seams as you sew.

3. Layout all the units and background pieces to form the block. Following the diagram, sew units into rows and rows into the complete block.

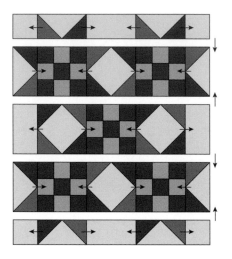

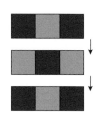

Add ¼" seam allowances.

Carpenter's Wheel Variation

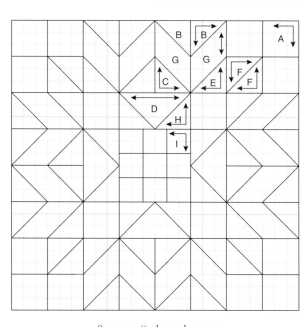

8 squares/inch graph paper

Vital Statistics

Drafting Category: Four-patch, 8 × 8 grid
Grid Dimension: ⅜", ½", ¾" for all shapes except inner nine-patch
Grid Dimension: Inner nine-patch, ¼", ½", the 4" block requires a template.
Number of Shapes: 5

Number of Pieces: 93
Techniques Used: Rotary Cutting—page 26, Double Half-Square Triangle Units—page 40, Templates—page 27, Square to Square—page 38, Oversize and Custom Cut—page 36, Strip Piecing—page 42.

Cutting

This block is constructed using squares and rectangles only, no triangles.

Shape A: Cut sixteen $7/8$", 1", $1 1/4$" squares from background fabric. Twelve are for the outer edge, four are for the corners of the inner Sawtooth star.

Shape B: Cut sixteen $7/8$", 1", $1 1/4$" squares from background.

Shape C: Cut eight $7/8$", 1", $1 1/4$" squares of background or second light fabric.

Shape D: Cut four $7/8$" × $1 1/4$", 1" × $1 1/2$", $1 1/4$" × 2" rectangles of background fabric.

Shape E: Cut eight $7/8$", 1", $1 1/4$" squares, four from dark block fabric and four from medium block fabric.

Shape F: Cut eight $1 1/4$", $1 1/2$", $1 3/4$" squares, four from dark block fabric and four from medium block fabric (oversized).

Shape G: Cut sixteen $7/8$" × $1 1/4$", 1" × $1 1/2$", $1 1/4$" × 2" rectangles, eight will be cut from the dark fabric, eight from the medium fabric.

Shape H: Cut eight $7/8$", 1", $1 1/4$" squares of star point fabric.

Shape I: Nine-patch: Cut three length grain strips $3/4$" × 6", 1" × 6" from a dark and from a medium light. The 4" block requires a template for the I Shapes or you could design something else for this 1" finished space, or you could cut a $1 1/2$" square from an interesting fabric.

Piecing Sequence and Pressing Path

This block has three different design areas, the outer star point area that surrounds the Sawtooth Star, the inner Sawtooth Star area and the Nine-patch area. Within each area are units. You will make units first, then lay out your block, evaluate it, and assemble. *Arrows and circles indicate pressing direction.*

Outer star point area

1. Make four FF Units using the Square-to-Square Technique—page 38 and the Oversize and Custom Cut Technique—page 36.

2. Custom cut a $7/8$", 1", $1 1/4$" square from each FF Unit. Make 4.

3. Join three A squares to each FF Unit.

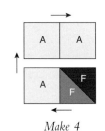

Make 4

Noteworthy

Work slowly, and pay close attention to correct fabric placement and direction of diagonal seam when making each unit. You will use the Double Half-Square Triangle Units technique—page 40 to create these units. It is helpful to make one of each unit and lay them out together to evaluate and use as a guide. Refer to photo and diagram often.

4. Make eight BGE Units, and eight BGC Units.

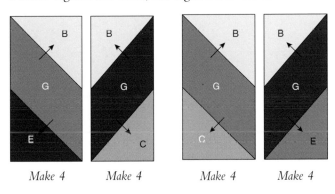

Make 4   *Make 4*   *Make 4*   *Make 4*

Inner Sawtooth Star area

1. Make four DHH Units. You will again use the Double Half-Square Triangle Units technique—page 40.

Make 4

Nine-patch Area–Shape I

2. Sew a dark-medium-dark strip unit and a medium-dark-medium strip unit. Carefully press after adding each strip, press all seams in one direction. Strip units should measure $1 1/4$", 2" wide. Trim seams if they are correct.

3. Cut two $3/4$", 1" segments from the dark-medium-dark strip unit and one $3/4$", 1" segment from the medium-dark-medium unit.

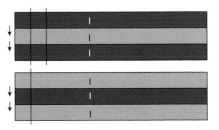

Arrange as shown, turning segments appropriately to create opposing seams from row to row.

4. Join the rows. The nine-patch unit should measure $1 1/4$", 2" square.

5. The 4" block requires the individual I squares sewn together to make a $1 1/2$" square.

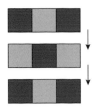

Block Assembly

1. Layout all units and examine carefully to be sure fabric and diagonals are appropriately positioned.
2. Assemble the inner Sawtooth Star first. It should measure 2", 2½", 3½" square.
3. Assemble the complete block as shown.

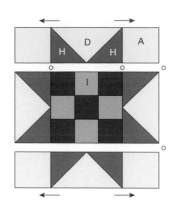

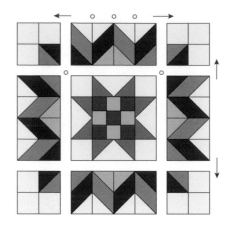

Add ¼" seam allowances.

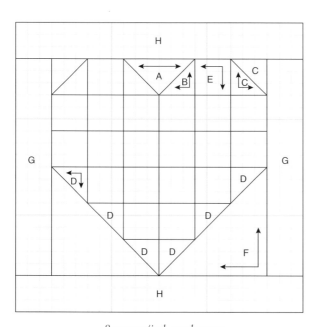

8 squares/inch graph paper

Vital Statistics

Drafting Category: Nine-patch, 6 × 6 grid
Grid Dimension: ⅜", ½", ⅞" (Sashing strips are not included in the grid)
Number of Shapes: 6 (B, C and D are all the same shape but are created differently)
Number of Pieces: 39
Techniques Used: Double Half-Square Triangle Units—page 40, Rotary Cutting—page 26, Sew and Flip—page 41, Mock-ups—page 23, Square-to-Square—page 38.

Cutting

Shape A: Cut one ⅞" × 1¼", 1" × 1½", 1⅜" × 2¼" rectangle from background fabric.
Shape B: Cut two ⅞", 1", 1⅜" squares from heart fabric.
Shape C: Cut two ⅞", 1", 1⅜" squares each from background and heart fabric.
Shape D: Cut six ⅞", 1", 1⅜" squares from heart fabric.
Shape E: Cut twenty ⅞", 1", 1⅜" squares of heart fabric.
Shape F: Cut one 2", 2⅜", 3½" square from background fabric, cut in half diagonally.
Shape G: Cut two ⅞" × 2¾", 1" × 3½", ⅞" × 5¾" rectangles from background fabric.
Shape H: Cut two ⅞" × 3½", 1" × 4½", ⅞" × 6½" rectangles from background fabric.

Piecing Sequence and Pressing Path

Arrows indicate pressing direction.

1. Make one ABB Unit referring to the Double Half-Square Triangle Units technique, page 40.

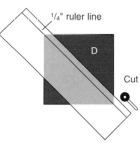

2. Make two CC Units, refer to Square-to-Square technique—page 38. Because there are only two, simply draw a diagonal line on the two lightest C squares and pair with the remaining C squares and sew just on the scrap side of the drawn line. Open the seam, measure to be sure the CC Unit is still the same size as the square you started with. Trim the seam.

Make 6

3. Cut each D square into a triangle by aligning the $1/4$" line of the ruler exactly through two opposite corners and cut.

Note: I cut the D triangle this way so the triangle edges line up with the square they are sewn to and eliminate the extended tips.

Noteworthy

Sashing strips are added to all sides of the heart to bring it up to the appropriate size. I do a rough cut mock-up of this block, composing each piece to get an accurate view of how the colors and fabrics relate to one another. It could be scrappy, one color, two colors, etc. When the composing is complete, I then cut the pieces for sewing. It is most important that you cut and sew accurately as well as sew very straight and press well. Maintaining the grid dimension ensures a well shaped heart.

4. Lay out all pieces and units of the heart and assemble in rows. Be very vigilant in maintaining the appropriate grid dimension. Keep the iron away from the bias edge of the D triangles.

5. Add the F triangles to the heart bottom. The heart should measure $2^3/4$", $3^1/2$", $5^3/4$" square.

6. Add the G sashing strips. Then add the H sashing strips.

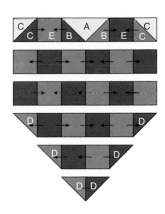

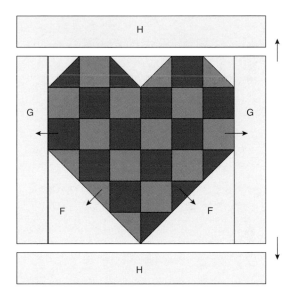

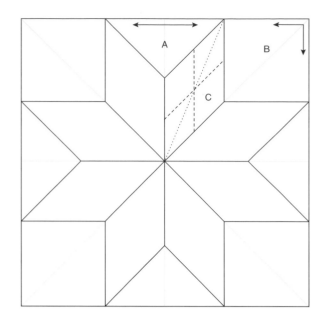

LeMoyne Star, Morning Star, Split-Diamond LeMoyne Star

Vital Statistics

Drafting Category: Eight Pointed Star

Grid Dimension: Use templates for all sizes to monitor sewing.

Number of Shapes: 3

Number of Pieces, LeMoyne Star: 16

Number of Pieces, Morning Star: 40

Number of Pieces, Split Diamond LeMoyne Star: 24

Techniques Used: Templates—page 27, Y-Seam Construction—page 41, Mirrors—page 23. Additionally, if doing Morning Star, Strip Piecing—page 42, Oversize and Custom Cut—page 36. Additionally, if doing the Split-Diamond LeMoyne Star, Strip Piecing—page 42.

Cutting

Shape A: Cut four from background fabric.

Shape B: Cut four from background fabric.

Shape C, LeMoyne Star: Cut eight from block fabric.

Shape C, Morning Star: Cut one 1" × 16", 1¼" × 30", 1¾" × 40" straight grain strip from both Fabric 1 and Fabric 3. Cut two 1" × 16", 1¼" × 30", 1¾" × 40" straight grain strips from Fabric 2.

Shape C, Split-Diamond LeMoyne Star: Cut one 1" × 20", 1½" × 24", 2" × 34" straight grain strip from two diamond fabrics.

Patterns are on page 122.

Piecing Sequence and Pressing Path LeMoyne Star

Arrows and circles indicate pressing direction.

1. Lay out all the pieces of the block.

2. Sew two C's to one A, begin at outer edge, sew to dot and backstitch. To do this you will sew with the A triangle on top once and then the C diamond on top. Sew the C diamonds together, begin at center, sew to dot and backstitch. Make four ACC Units.

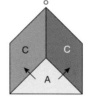

Make 4

3. Sew a B square to the right side of each ACC Unit. Sew from the edge to the dot and backstitch. The B square will be on top, do not press at this time.

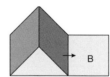

Make 4

4. Join two ABCC Units together by first sewing the B to C from the edge to the dot and backstitch; B will be on top. Join the diamonds from the center edge to the dot and backstitch.

5. Join the two halves. Sew the two B squares, one at a time, to the C diamonds from the edge to the dot and backstitch. The center seam is sewn last. Carefully match the center with an alignment pin; pin at the two dots at either end of the seam. It is important that the two halves have a distinct V shape where the three seams join; and that you have a ¼" seam allowance from the bottom of the V to the edge. If you do not have two accurate halves, you will

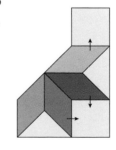

Make 2

not get an accurate whole star. If you are unsure of matching the center, increase your stitch length and machine baste the center area only and check it. When it meets your standards, resew with a smaller stitch length.

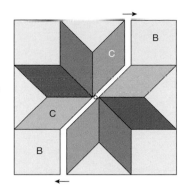

The Morning Star

This block is exactly the same as the simple LeMoyne Star block except that each of the eight diamonds are fragmented (denoted by dashed lines) into four smaller diamonds resulting in 32 diamonds total instead of eight. The eight C diamonds (four-patches on slant) will be created oversized, and you will then use the C template with appropriate lines drawn on it to custom cut the exact size diamonds. The Morning Star has three positions of color. Position 1 fabric/color congregates in the center and creates a very small LeMoyne Star.

The more solid the fabric the more discrepancies will show, the busier the fabric the more forgiving. Position 2 fabric/color is used twice as much as 1 and 3 and therefore is dominant. It also creates a continuous circle around the small center star. Position 3 fabric/color are the tips and will touch the background so you must create contrast to see them.

Piecing Sequence and Pressing Path for Morning Star

When all eight C diamonds are created, refer to the LeMoyne Star for assembly instructions.

1. Sew Fabric 1 and 2 strips together lengthwise, offsetting by the width of the strip, press seam open. Sew Fabric 2 and 3 together similarly.

2. With fabric strips right side up as shown, develop a 45° angle on the end of each strip unit and cut eight 1", 1¼", 1¾" slices

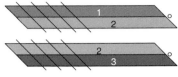

Cut 8 slices from each

from each unit. To maintain the correct angle, always keep the 45° line of the ruler on the seam and the dimension line of the ruler you are cutting on the edge of the fabric. When you cannot place the two lines appropriately, reestablish the angle.

3. Take a slice from each strip unit, arrange them in different orientations and on different background fabrics using the mirrors to interview fabric choices.

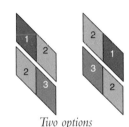

Two options

4. When you have decided on the arrangement you prefer, focus on making one diamond at a time. Pick up two slices, one from each strip unit, and form the diamond. Place the two slices right sides together, being aware of what edges will get sewn.

5. Make a mark ¼" down from the eventual sewn edge over the seam. Turn the pair over and make a mark on the other slice similarly.

6. Using an alignment pin, pin through the mark on the open seam of the slice fac-

ing you and into the mark and open seam of the other slice. The pin must travel through the open seam area, not through either fabric. The alignment pin will help rest one slice onto another, align the edges, and match the marks. Place a pin at each end. Place an additional pin, placed as shown, just next to the alignment pin and remove the alignment pin. The alignment pin does not secure the intersection, it aligns it only.

7. Sew the paired slices together, sewing across the mark. You can also draw a ¹/₄" sewing line all the way across, although you must still mark and match the center intersection with the alignment pin. See page 48 if your intersection does not match.

8. When the intersection is matched, press the seam open 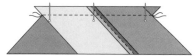 and trim. Repeat for the remaining seven diamonds.

9. These eight diamonds are oversized and must now be custom cut to the appropriate size. Place the C template (which has appropriate markings) face up on the right side of each diamond, aligning center and seam lines with lines on the template. Trace around the template but do not mark dots on the right side of the fabric. Cut out the diamond shape, cutting the line off. Turn fabric diamond over, and place C template face down to mark the dots. Be sure to use a marking tool that does not bleed to the right side of your fabric. The eight diamonds are now the correct size to sew the block together, refer to the LeMoyne Star instructions.

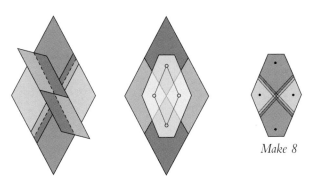

Make 8

Noteworthy

Because eight or sixteen seams meet in the center of the star and the diamond seams will be pressed open, be sure to use a little smaller stitch length and a well camouflaged thread color to eliminate the chance of thread showing. You can use an interesting printed fabric or border print and use the C shape template to create a whole design by cutting the exact same area from a fabric eight times, page 28.

For the Morning Star block, I cut out the diamond and then mark the dots in two steps because I can see more clearly from the right side to match the templates lines to the seam lines; then turn the diamond over to mark the dots. If you can see clearly from the wrong side of the diamond, you can trace the shape and mark the dots all in one step with template C face down.

The Split-Diamond LeMoyne Star

This block is exactly the same as the simple LeMoyne Star except that each of the eight diamonds are split in length half lengthwise (denoted by dotted lines). To make the C-split diamonds appear to have dimension you must choose two fabrics that create high contrast between them. This is a challenging block as there are sixteen seams that must meet exactly in the center.

Piecing Sequence and Pressing Path for the Split-Diamond LeMoyne Star

When all eight C split-diamonds are created, refer to LeMoyne Star for assembly instructions.

1. Sew the two shape C strips (one dark, one light) together down the length, open the seam and trim.

2. Place the C template, face down on the wrong side of the strip unit, aligning the seam with the line on the template, trace, mark dots and cut out. Repeat seven times.

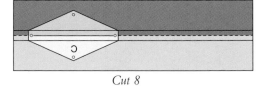

Cut 8

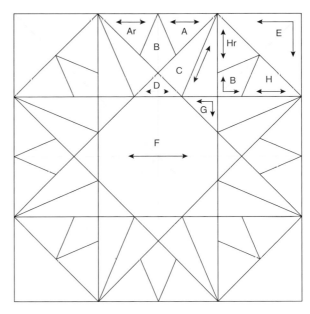

Vital Statistics

Drafting Category: Eight Pointed Star
Grid Dimension: Use templates for all sizes to monitor sewing.
Number of Shapes: 6
Number of Pieces: 53
Techniques Used: Templates—page 27, Strip Piecing—page 42.

Cutting

All shapes in all sizes require templates. Patterns are on page 120.
Shape A and Ar: Cut four each from background fabric.
Shape B: Cut eight from block fabric.
★Shape C: Cut eight from block fabric.
Shape D: Cut four from block fabric.
Shape E: Cut four from background fabric.

Shape F: Cut one from block fabric.
Shape G: Cut four from block fabric.
Shape H and Hr: Cut four each from background fabric.
★*Cut two straight-grain strips of block fabric, one medium, and one dark 1" × 20", 1¹/₄" × 20", 1¹/₂" × 25". Pair the two strips and sew down the length, press the seam open and trim. Place the C template face down on the wrong side of the strip unit, aligning seam to line on template. Be consistent with your placement or the medium and dark fabrics could change sides! Trace and make dots eight times, cut the shapes out. Refer to Five Pointed Star—page 98.*

Piecing Sequence and Pressing Path

Arrows indicate pressing direction.

  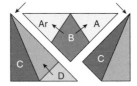

Unit 1–Make 4   *Unit 2–Make 4*   *Unit 3–Make 1*

Sew four of Unit 1, four of Unit 2, and one of Unit 3, pinning at dots for proper alignment of fabric pieces but sewing edge to edge.
Make only one of each unit and evaluate for accuracy first before continuing to assemble the complete block.

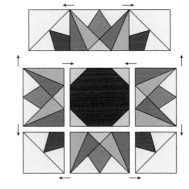

Noteworthy

Shape C will be created from a template and two different fabrics strips, one medium and one very dark, to create depth. One approach to color choice would be to think of the block as two different stars, one created from the C points and one from the smaller B points. The D and G triangles are small and benefit from being light or bright. Shape F is large and could use a larger printed fabric, perhaps custom cut. Although A and Ar and H and Hr are the same shape, they require the straight of grain on different edges, so to create less confusion, make a template for each and keep them separate. This is true for Shapes D and G as well. Be sure to place them in the block correctly.

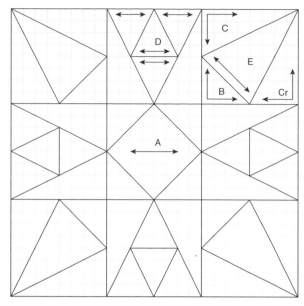

8 squares/inch graph paper

Vital Statistics

Drafting Category: Nine-patch, 6 × 6 grid
Grid Dimension: $1/2$", 1"
Number of Shapes: 5
Number of Pieces: 45
Techniques Used: Templates—page 27.

Cutting

All shapes in all sizes require templates. Patterns on page 120.
Shape A: Cut one from block fabric.
Shape B: Cut eight from block fabric.
Shape C and Cr: Cut four each from both background and block fabrics.
Shape D: Cut eight from both background and block fabric.
Shape E: Cut four from block fabric.

Noteworthy

This is a beautiful block with lots of opportunity for color and value change. I suggest doing a rough cut mock-up before cutting and sewing. When piecing this block be aware of what edge of the D triangle is straight grain and keep it in the correct position in the block. The three edges of this shape appear to all be equal, but in actuality the grain arrow edge is slightly shorter than the remaining two edges that are equal to each other.

Piecing Sequence and Pressing Path

Arrows indicate pressing direction.

1. This block is sewn in three units. Four of Unit 1, four of Unit 2, and one of Unit 3. Make one of each unit first, measure and/or monitor with templates before continuing. Individual units should measure $1^1/2$", $2^1/2$". The 4" block requires templates for all monitoring.
2. Join units.
3. Join units into rows; join rows into the completed block.

Unit 1–Make 4

Unit 2–Make 4

Unit 3-Make 1

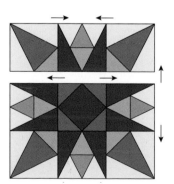

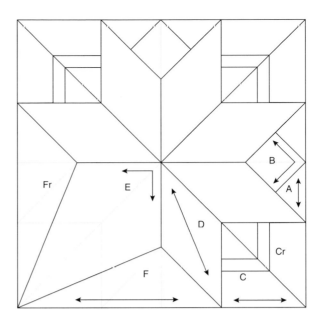

Vital Statistics

Drafting Category: Eight Pointed Star

Grid Dimension: Use templates for all sizes to monitor sewing.

Number of Shapes: 8

Number of Pieces: 33

Techniques Used: Strip Piecing—page 42, Rotary Cutting—page 26, Templates—page 27, Mirrors—page 23, Very Narrow Borders—page 45, Y-Seam Construction—page 41.

Cutting

Make templates for Shapes B,C,D,E,F for all block sizes. The 4" block requires an additional template for Shape A; cut four from background fabric. Patterns are on page 122.

Shape A: Cut one 1⅞", 2½" square from background fabric, cut into quarters diagonally.

Shape B: Cut two from block fabric.

★Shape C and Cr: Cut three of each from a strip unit.

Shape D: Cut six from block fabric.

Shape E: Cut one from block fabric.

Shape F and Fr: Cut one of each from background fabric.

★Shape C and Cr, for all blocks, is created by making a three strip unit and tracing the C-template on the right side of the strip unit, face up three times and face down three times, aligning seam lines to lines on template. Now turn cut shapes over and mark the dots on the wrong side of the fabric.

Fabric 1: Cut one strip 1½" × 16", 1½" × 16", 1¾" × 20" from Shape B square fabric.

Fabric 2: Cut one strip 1" × 16", 1" × 16", ¾" × 20" from sparkle fabric.

Fabric 3: Cut one strip 1¾" × 16", 1¾" × 16", 2¼" × 20" from background fabric.

3" and 4" Block: Join 1 to 2, trim seam allowance to an exact ⅛", press seam to 2. Join 1-2 to 3 with 1-2 on top. Match edges but sew just next to the trimmed seam allowance. Trim seam to a generous 1/8" from last line of stitches, press to 3.

6" Block: Join 1 to 2, press seam to 2. Join 1-2 to 3, 1-2 on top. Sew with a ¼" seam allowance, press to 3. Place the C template on the wrong side of the strip unit, matching one of the seams to a line on the template consistently. Place the template face down three times and face up three times.

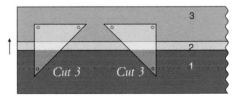

Noteworthy

Take advantage of having templates. Find an interesting fabric for the D diamond that creates the bouquet. Use the mirrors to interview fabrics and colors. Add the sparkle in the narrow strip in the corners. Shape E is a large piece, make the fabric great or fracture the space to create additional design.

Piecing Sequence and Pressing Path

Arrows indicate pressing direction.

1. Lay out the pieces of the block.
2. Make two AAB Units. When units are complete, make $1/4$" reference dot on shape B.
3. Lay out block again, assemble as shown. Dots indicate Y-seam areas.

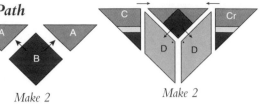

Make 2

Make 2

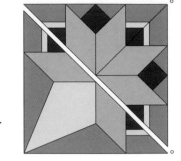

Carnival Ride

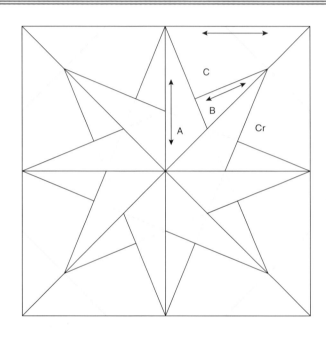

Vital Statistics

Drafting Category: Eight Pointed Star
Grid Dimension: Use templates for all sizes to monitor sewing.
Number of Shapes: 3
Number of Pieces: 24
Techniques Used: Templates—page 27.

Cutting

All shapes in all sizes require templates.
Patterns are on page 121.
Shape A: Cut eight from medium block fabric.
Shape B: Cut eight from dark block fabric.
Shape C and Cr: Cut four each from background fabric.

Piecing Sequence and Pressing Path

You will mark and pin at the dots, but sewing will be from edge to edge. *Arrows and circles indicate pressing direction.*

1. You will create four quadrants, one at a time. Each quadrant should measure 2", $2^1/2$", $3^1/2$".
Note: B is added to C and Cr on different edges. Be aware.
2. Lay out the four quadrants and assemble.

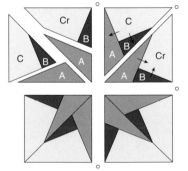

Noteworthy

Making the B shape very dark allows it to recede and create the illusion of depth.

Block design by Sally Collins

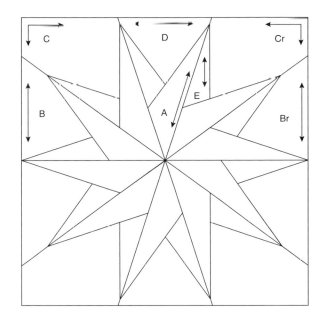

Vital Statistics

Drafting Category: Ten equal divisions of a circle (36° each)

Grid Dimension: Use templates for all sizes to monitor sewing.

Number of Shapes: 5

Number of Pieces: 30

Techniques Used: Templates—page 27, Mirrors—page 23.

Cutting

All sizes require templates. Patterns are on page 121.

Shape A: Cut ten from star point fabric.

Shape B and Br: Cut two of each from background fabric.

Shape C and Cr: Cut two of each from background fabric.

Shape D: Cut two from background fabric.

Shape E: Cut ten from dark star point fabric.

Piecing Sequence and Pressing Path

Arrows indicate pressing direction.

Notice that only the two horizontal points touch the edge of the block.

1. Layout the block and assemble one half of the block in five sections. Repeat for the second half.

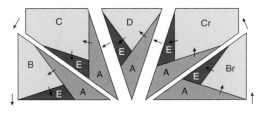

Make 2 halves

2. Join the two halves, press this long seam open in the middle area, clip and press in direction of arrows at the two ends of the seam.

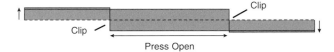

Noteworthy

Although you will pin at the dots to align pieces, you will always sew edge to edge. Be sure you clearly see your sewing path. Handle cut fabric pieces very carefully as there are many exposed bias edges. Finger press most of the time and use your iron with care and caution. There needs to be highly exaggerated contrast between Shapes A and E to clarify the star design. You can use two values of one color, or use two values of five different colors twice, or two values of two colors and place them alternately. Remember simple is always best! If you place the A template on a plaid fabric in the same place ten times you will develop a design. Use your mirrors to interview.

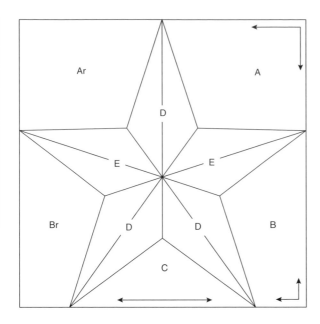

Five Pointed Star

Vital Statistics

Grid Dimension: Use templates to monitor sewing.
Number of Shapes: 5
Number of Pieces: 15
Techniques Used: Templates—page 27, Y-Seam Construction—page 41.

Cutting

Make accurate templates for all shapes and all block sizes, transferring line on D/E shapes to template to aid placement on fabric strip unit. Patterns are on page 123.

Shape A and Ar: Cut one each from background fabric.
Shape B and Br: Cut one each from background fabric.
Shape C : Cut one from background fabric.
Shape D and E: Cut from block fabric strip unit. To make strip unit for D/E shapes, cut one 1" × 15", 1½" × 20", 2" × 30" straight grain strips from two highly contrasted star point fabrics. Position them right sides together. Using a well-blended thread color and a small stitch length, sew down the length with a ¼" seam allowance. Press the seam open and trim. Place the D/E templates face down on the wrong side of the strip unit, aligning line on template with seam. Trace and cut out five times.

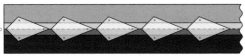

Cut 3 D shapes and 2 E shapes.

Piecing Sequence and Pressing Path

Arrows and circle indicate pressing direction.

Due to many bias edges, handle and press pieces carefully.
1. Join A and Ar to each side of D. Sew from the outer edge of the block to the dot and backstitch. Press away from D and trim.

2. Sew an E to B and an E to Br from outer edge to dot and backstitch. Press away from E and trim.
3. Sew a D to each side of C from outer edge to dot and backstitch. Press away from D and trim. Join D edges, dot to dot and backstitching at each dot. Do not press or trim.
4. Join AArD to EB from outer edge to dot and backstitch. Now join D/E edges, dot to dot and backstitching at each dot. Do not trim or press yet. Add EBr Unit to other side of AArD Unit similarly. You now have AArBBrDEE sewn together.
5. Add DDC Unit to B and Br, sewing from edge to dot and backstitching. Now join D/E edges, sewing from dot to dot and backstitching at each dot. Evaluate and critique center intersection carefully. Press D/E seams in one direction and trim.

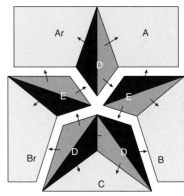

Note D and E placement.

Noteworthy

The D and E shapes must be placed in the block exactly as diagramed. You could simplify it somewhat by leaving the D/E shape unsplit, but you will lose character.
Making accurate templates and punching holes to indicate matching points on fabric is vital to the success of this block. To create dimension in the star points, exaggerate the contrast of the two fabrics when splitting the D/E shape.

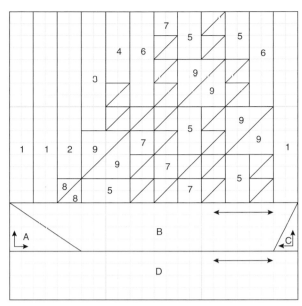

Block design by Sally Collins

Vital Statistics

Drafting Category: Miscellaneous

Grid Dimension: The 3" block is created on a $1/4$" grid and the 6" block on a $1/2$" grid.

Number of Shapes: 13

Number of Pieces: 73

Techniques Used: Bias Strip—page 37, Templates—page 27, Rotary Cutting—page 26.

Cutting

The 4" block requires templates for all shapes. Patterns are on page 123.

Shape 1: Cut three $3/4$" × $2^1/2$", 1" × $4^1/2$" rectangles from sky fabric.

Shape 2: Cut one $3/4$" × $2^1/4$", 1" × 4" rectangle from sky fabric.

Shape 3: Cut one $3/4$" × $1^3/4$", 1" × 3" rectangle from sky fabric.

Shape 4: Cut one $3/4$" × $1^1/4$", 1" × 2" rectangle from sky fabric.

Shape 5: Cut five $3/4$" × 1", 1" × $1^1/2$" rectangles from sky fabric.

Shape 6: Cut two $3/4$" × $1^1/2$", 1" × $2^1/2$" rectangles from sky fabric.

Shape 7: Cut four $3/4$", 1" squares from sky fabric.

★Shape 8: Cut twenty-three $3/4$", 1" half-square triangle units of both sky and sail fabric.

★Shape 9: Cut three 1", $1^1/2$" half-square triangle units consisting of both sky and sail fabric.

★*Shapes 8 and 9 are two different sizes of half-square triangle units. They will be created using the Bias Strip technique—page 37. Shapes 8 and 9 for the 4" block will be made from the Bias Strip technique, but cut the units using two square templates the size of each unit.*

Cut one $1^1/2$" × 30", $1^1/2$" × 30", 2" × 40" bias strip from both sky and sail fabric. The strip lengths are the total number of inches needed, multiple strips of shorter lengths could be used as well.

Shape A: Cut one from sky fabric.

Shape B: Cut one from ship fabric.

Shape C: Cut one from sky fabric.

Shape D: Cut one 1" × $3^1/2$", $1^1/2$" × $6^1/2$" rectangle from water fabric.

Noteworthy

This block is created in three sections: the sky/sail section, the ship/sky section, and the water section. It is most important that you sew very straight and maintain the grid dimension. You must constantly monitor your sewing for accuracy, especially in the sky/sail section. I suggest choosing one sail fabric and one sky fabric for ease of cutting. The ship/sky section requires templates for all block sizes. Although the water section is a rectangle, I had a "watery" fabric and chose to appliqué the water onto the block for a more realistic look.

Piecing Sequence and Pressing Path

Arrows and circles indicate pressing direction.
Assemble the three separate sections, then join the sections to complete the block.

Note: I cannot over emphasize the need to maintain the grid, sew very straight and proceed slowly.

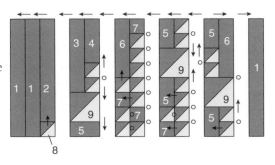

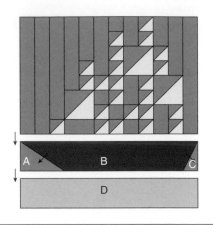

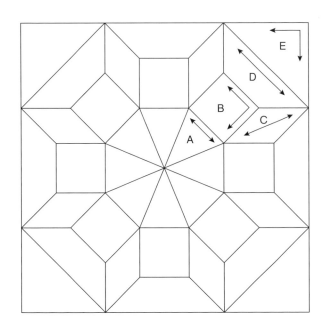

Vital Statistics

Drafting Category: Eight Pointed Star
Grid Dimension: Use templates for all sizes to monitor sewing.
Number of Shapes: 5
Number of Pieces: 36
Techniques Used: Y-Seam Construction—page 41, Templates—page 27, Mirrors—page 23.

Cutting

Make templates for all shapes. Patterns are on page 122.
Shape A: Cut eight for the center octagon from block fabric (pie shape).
Shape B: Cut eight from block fabric (square).
Shape C: Cut eight from block fabric (diamond).
Shape D: Cut eight from block fabric (trapezoid).
Shape E: Cut four from background (triangle).

Piecing Sequence and Pressing Path

Edge-to-edge sewing in the center octagon and at the outer edges only. All other seams are y-seams and require backstitching at the beginning and end of the sewing line and then removal from the machine to reposition. *Arrow and circles indicate pressing direction.*

1. Lay out the block, evaluate and make any changes necessary.
2. Make two center octagon units. Pin at the dots for proper alignment, but sew from edge to edge.

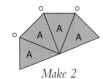

Make 2

3. Make four corner units. Sew a C diamond to each side of a B square. Sew dot to dot. Evaluate only, do not press. Add D trapezoid to B square first, dot to dot. Then reposition and sew D to both C's, from outer edge to dot. Add E triangle, pinning at dots for proper alignment, but sewing edge to edge. Press carefully. Make three more corner units. Do not place iron near the bias edges.

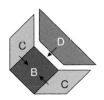 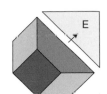

Make 4

4. Lay out block again. From this point on, carefully finger press only, in direction of arrows. Press with iron when block is complete.

5. Sew two B squares to each octagon unit, dot to dot.

6. Sew two corner units to each octagon unit by joining B edge to A edge, dot to dot. Reposition and sew B edge to C edge, dot to dot.

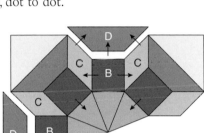

Make 2

7. Sew two D trapezoids to each octagon unit by joining B edge to D edge, dot to dot. Then join D edge to C.

8. Join the two halves.

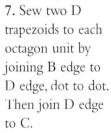

Make 2

Noteworthy

Clearly understand the concept of y-seaming and the importance of not sewing into the seam allowance. Know which dots are y-seams and which dots are not. This is a slow, choppy block to sew; take your time. Take advantage of using templates and use your fabric prints cleverly. Decide what element in the block you want to emphasize the most or least (star points, center, etc.) and that will help you decide value placement. Use mirrors to design center octagon by placing them around just one pie shape placed on an interesting fabric. Think about what the edge will eventually touch relevant to value and color when choosing shape D fabric print and color.

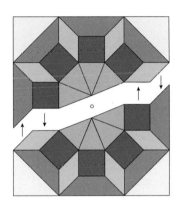

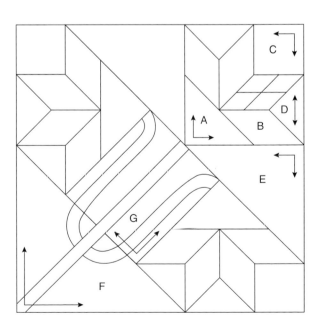

North Carolina Lily

Vital Statistics

Drafting Category: Eight Pointed Star
Grid Dimension: Use templates for all sizes to monitor sewing.

Number of Shapes: 8 including stem
Number of Pieces: 29 (65 if fracturing diamond) including stem

Techniques Used: Templates—page 27, Metal Bias Bar—page 42, Y-Seam Construction—page 41. Additionally, if fracturing the diamond, Rotary Cutting—page 26, Strip Piecing—page 42, Oversize and Custom Cut—page 36.

Cutting

Make accurate templates for all shapes A through G. Transfer lines onto template Shape B if fracturing. Patterns are on page 124.

Shape A: Cut three from block fabric.

★Shape B: Cut twelve from block fabric. (You can leave this shape whole or fracture it.)

Shape C: Cut three from background fabric.

Shape D: Cut six from background fabric.

Shape E: Cut two from background fabric.

Shape F: Cut one from background fabric.

Shape G: Cut one from background fabric.

Stem: 3" and 4" block, cut one bias strip $7/8$" × 12" and use the $1/8$" metal bias bar.

Stem: 6" block, cut one bias strip 1" × 7" and one bias strip 1" × 10" and use the $1/4$" metal bias bar.

★Shape B can be fractured as follows: Cut one strip from Fabrics 1 and 3 and two strips from Fabric 2, each 1" × 20" on the straight of grain. This size of strip will accommodate all block sizes. Refer to Morning Star—page 91–92 Steps 1–9, to make twelve diamonds.

Noteworthy

It is important to clearly understand the Y-seam construction concept and the importance of not sewing into the seam allowance. Know which dots are Y-seams and which dots are not. This is a slow, choppy block to sew, take your time. There are a lot of pieces and opportunities for color. The three flowers could all be the same or each different. Cut small diamonds and interview fabric and color using the mirrors. Fracturing the diamonds will create more interest and design detail.

Piecing Sequence and Pressing Path

Arrows indicate pressing direction.

This block is somewhat challenging, so take time with it. You will sew three flower units together, then join those with additional background pieces and bias stem to complete the block. Notice that Shape D and C placement changes in each of the three flower units. Make one at a time.

1. Make three Flower Units as shown.

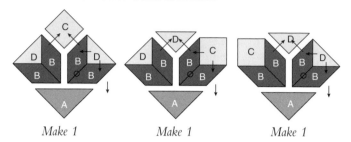

Make 1   Make 1   Make 1

2. Lay out block with background fabric.

3. Make the bias stem referring to Metal Bias Bars—page 42. The $7/8$" × 12" bias for the 3" and 4" block should be cut in half.

4. Assemble the block as shown, inserting ends of bias on Shape G where indicated. Let the bias "dangle" as you continue to assemble the block.

5. Make appropriate reference marks for positioning bias on Shapes F and G, glue-baste in place and hand appliqué stem edges to finish.

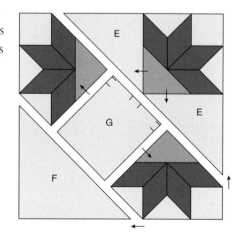

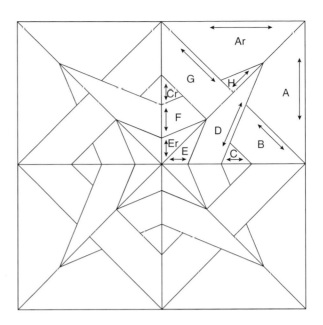

Vital Statistics

Drafting Category: Eight Pointed Star
Grid Dimension: Use templates to monitor sewing.
Number of Shapes: 8
Number of Pieces: 44
Techniques Used: Templates—page 27.

Cutting

Make templates for all block sizes and all shapes. Patterns are on page 124.

Shape A and Ar: Cut four each from background fabric.
Shape B: Cut four from block fabric.
Shape C and Cr: Cut four each from background fabric.
Shape D: Cut four from block fabric.
Shape E and Er: Cut four each from block fabric.
Shape F: Cut four from block fabric.
Shape G: Cut four from block fabric.
Shape H: Cut four from block fabric.

Noteworthy

This is a challenging block, especially in the 3" size. There are three distinct design areas. Working from the center out, the E and Er shapes create a split four pointed star, so using two highly contrasted values of one color will create dimension. The D, F, and H shapes create the second star and, again, two highly contrasted values of one color work well. The G and B shapes form a somewhat woven or over/under square on point, and here a narrow border print or one color works well. You will create four quadrants, each made from two halves. These are very small pieces if you are doing the 3" size. Take your time, the dots will help to align the shapes onto one another properly, but you will always sew from edge to edge.

Piecing Sequence and Pressing Path

Arrows and circles indicate pressing direction.
You will use the dots for properly aligning one piece onto another, but you will always sew edge to edge. Use templates to monitor accuracy before trimming.

1. Layout pieces and focus on creating one quadrant at a time. Make four quadrants.
2. Layout all four quadrants. Join two quadrants twice, open the seam, evaluate and trim seam.
3. Join the two halves of the block, open the seam, evaluate and trim seam.

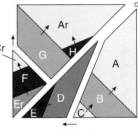

Make 4

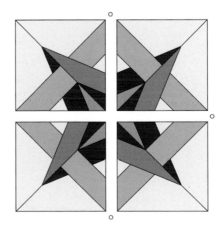

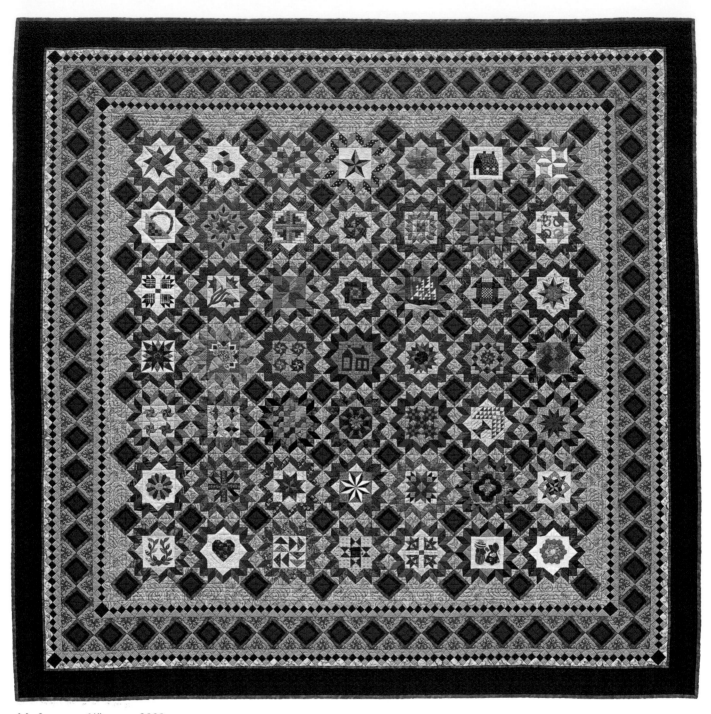

My Journey, *61" square, 2000.*

VIII Quilt—My Journey

Sampler quilts have always been a favorite style of mine because they offer a variety of color, design, technical learning and exploring opportunities. The featured quilt is titled *My Journey* and is approximately 61" square. It is a culmination and an accumulation of twenty years of growth, classes, experience, progress, books, trials, errors, successes, and failures. It is a quilt that embodies what I love most in quiltmaking: precision sewing, small scale piecing, and traditional style patchwork blocks.

This quilt is a collection of forty-nine different 3" square traditional-style patchwork and appliqué blocks that range in skill level from easy to advanced. This kind of work is not difficult, although it often takes more time and patience to accomplish. All piecing is done on the sewing machine, using various methods and techniques with 1/4" seam allowances. No foundation piecing is used. Over the years I accumulated a little stack of 3" blocks from teaching and personal experimenting and had often thought how wonderful it would be to create a large quilt from small blocks. For this quilt I added new blocks to the ones I already had to total forty-nine. I placed the 3" blocks into the center of a constant 6" "host" block to give the small ones more importance. This host block serves to equalize the blocks so no one single block is more important than any other; they all need each other and together create a oneness. The host block also enhances each small block in color and fabric to become its frame. Combining the variety of sampler blocks with the repetition of the host block gives balance and harmony to the quilt.

Adding a corner design element creates a secondary design that integrates the blocks so the quilt becomes somewhat tapestry-like. A completer border (completes the corner design detail of the twenty-four outside blocks), and three-pieced borders echo color and design from the body of the quilt, and a final multiple fabric border frames the quilt and brings it to conclusion. Enjoy *My Journey*.

Instructions

Throughout these instructions the letters indicate shape identification, the numbers indicate fabric identification. To make this quilt as shown you will first make the forty-nine 3" sampler blocks. Then make the 6" host block units and join those units to each sampler block. Next you will add the design detail onto the four corners of each host block. After joining all forty-nine blocks together, you'll add the completer border, three separate pieced borders, and a final multiple strip border.

Fabric Requirements

I consistently used Fabrics 1 through 8. Fabrics 9, 10, and 11 change for each host block depending on your color and fabric choices used for each individual sampler block. Yardage amounts are for the quilt shown only. If you are increasing the size of this quilt, yardage amounts and cutting dimensions will need to be adjusted.

Fabric 1: Beige Background 2 1/2 yards
Fabric 2: Teal 3 1/4 yards, includes binding
Fabric 3: Dark Burgundy 3 1/4 yards
Fabric 4: Medium Burgundy 2/3 yard
Fabric 5: Beige Stripe 1/2 yard
Fabric 6: Beige Pin Dot 1/2 yard
Fabric 7: Beige Print 2/3 yard or 144 repeats on a border print
Fabric 8: Beige Floral 1/3 yard
Fabric 9: Host Block Dark 1/8 yard per 6" block
Fabric 10: Host Block Medium 1/8 yard per 6" block
Fabric 11: Host Block Light 1/8 yard per 6" block

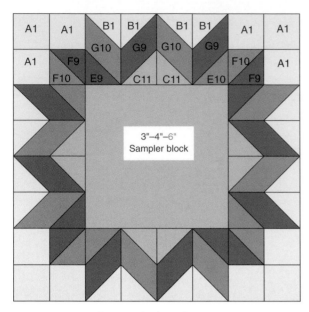

8 squares/inch graph paper

Host Block

The following information includes cutting requirements for making one 6", 8" and 12" host block that accommodates a 3", 4", and 6" sampler block.

Drafting Category: Four-patch, 8 x 8 grid.
Grid Dimension: $3/4$", 1", $1^1/2$"
Number of Shapes: 2 (only squares and rectangles)
Number of Pieces: 68
Techniques Used: Double Half-Square Triangle Units—page 40, Square to Square—page 38, Oversize and Custom Cut—page 36.

Cutting

Shape A: Cut twelve $1^1/4$", $1^1/2$", 2" squares from Fabric 1 (corners).
Shape B: Cut sixteen $1^1/4$", $1^1/2$", 2" squares from Fabric 1 (edge triangles).
Shape C: Cut eight $1^1/4$", $1^1/2$", 2" squares from Fabric 11.
There is no Shape D.
Shape E: Cut eight $1^1/4$", $1^1/2$", 2" squares, four from Fabric 9 and four from Fabric 10.
Shape F: Cut eight $1^3/4$", 2", $2^1/2$" squares, (oversized) four from Fabric 9, and four from Fabric 10.
Shape G: Cut sixteen$1^1/4$" × 2", $1^1/2$" × $2^1/2$", 2" × $3^1/2$" rectangles, eight from Fabric 9, eight from Fabric 10.

Host Block Units

1. Make eight BGE Units and eight BGC Units following the Double Half-Square Triangle Units technique on page 40. Pay close attention to the direction of the diagonal when sewing and keep the dark and medium fabrics in their proper positions. Individual completed units should measure the same size as the Shape G rectangle you start with.

2. Join two BGE and two BGC Units together as shown, four times.

3. Make four FF Units using the Square-to-Square and Oversize and Custom Cut techniques—pages 36, 38.

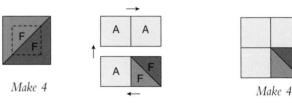

Make 4

Custom cut a $1^1/4$", $1^1/2$", 2" square from each pairing.
4. Join three A squares to one FF Unit four times.

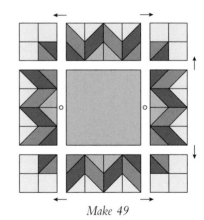

Make 4

Make 4

5. Lay out all the Host Block Units around a sampler block and assemble. Repeat for the remaining 48 sampler blocks.

Make 49

Corner Design

Cutting is for adding the corner design to one 6" block that accommodates a 3" sampler block only. Adding the corner design element is simple in concept, but you must sew very straight and always keep a sense of squareness.

Shape H: Cut four $3/4$" × $3^1/2$" strips from Fabric 2 (196 for all 49).
Shape I: Cut two $2^1/2$" squares from Fabric 3, cut in half diagonally (98 for all 49).
Shape J: Cut two 2" squares from Fabric 4, cut in half diagonally (98 for all 49).

1. Draw a diagonal line (chalk) $1/4$" from the corner points on the right side of the fabric. Align and center the edge of the Fabric 2 strip (Shape H), right sides together, to the drawn line and sew with a $1/4$" seam allowance. Trim off the background corner. Press strip seam allowance to corner.

2. Sew a Fabric 3 Shape I triangle to the Fabric 2 Shape H strip, aligning edges. Press seam allowance to corner.

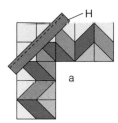

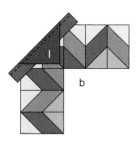 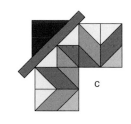

3. Draw a chalk line $1/2$" from the last seam sewn on the right side of the fabric. Align the Fabric 4 Shape J triangle edge, right sides together, to the drawn line and sew. Trim Fabric 3 Shape I excess to $1/4$" of the last line of stitching, press to corner. Repeat for all four corners.

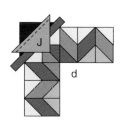 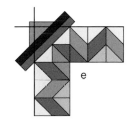 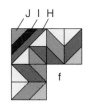

4. Trim excess to edge of block ($6^1/2$" square).
5. Arrange and join together the 49 blocks to create the body of the quilt, $42^1/2$" square.

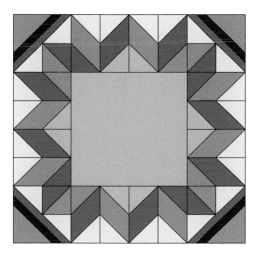

Completer Border–Unit 1

Shape K: Cut twenty-eight 2" × $6^1/2$" rectangles from background Fabric 1.
Shape H: Cut fifty-six $3/4$" × $3^1/2$" strips from Fabric 2.
Shape I: Cut twenty-eight $2^1/2$" squares from Fabric 3, cut in half diagonally.
Shape J: Cut twenty-eight 2" squares from Fabric 4, cut in half diagonally.

Imagine a 2" square at each end of Shape K and draw a diagonal line $1/4$" from an imaginary corner to corner line. Following Corner Design steps 1 through 4 exactly, create 28 Complete Border Unit 1's.

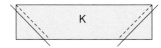 

Make 28 Unit 1's

Completer Border–Corner Unit 2

Shape L: Cut four 2" squares from background Fabric 1.
Shape H: Cut four $3/4$" × $3^1/2$" strips from Fabric 2.
Shape I: Cut two $2^1/2$" squares from Fabric 3, cut in half diagonally.
Shape J: Cut two 2" squares from Fabric 4, cut in half diagonally.

1. Following the Corner Design steps 1 through 4 exactly, create four Completer Border Corner Unit 2's.
2. Join seven Unit 1's together four times. Add two borders to the two sides of the quilt.
3. Add a Unit 2 to each end of the two remaining completer borders and add to the top and bottom of the quilt.

Make 4 Unit 2's

Pieced Border 1 and 3

Border 3 information is in parentheses.

Note: The cutting and assembly instruction for Border 1 and 3 are given together, but obviously you will add Border 2 in between them!

To make 120 (144) Four-Patch Unit 3's:
Cut four (five) $1^1/4$" × 40" strips from Fabric 3.
Cut four (five) $1^1/4$" × 40" strips from Fabric 5.

To cut 240 (288) quarter-square triangles:
Shape M: Cut thirty (thirty-six), $2^3/4$" squares from Fabric 1 (6); cut into quarters diagonally.
Shape M: Cut thirty (thirty-six), $2^3/4$" squares from Fabric 6 (8); cut into quarters diagonally.

To cut 16 half-square triangles.

Shape N: Cut two $1^5/_8$" squares from Fabric 1 (6); cut in half diagonally.

Shape N: Cut six $1^5/_8$" squares from Fabric 6 (8); cut in half diagonally.

To cut the plain corner squares Unit 4, cut eight using Template X from Fabric 3.

Four-Patch Unit 3 Assembly

1. Sew one Fabric 3 and one Fabric 5 strip together four (five) times, press seam to dark.

2. Develop a straight edge and cut 240 (288) $1^1/_4$" segments.

3. Sew two segments together 120 (144) times.

4. Using Template X, custom cut 120 (144) accurate Four-Patch Units.

Pieced Border 1 and 3 Assembly

1. For one side border join Four-Patch Unit 3, and triangles M and N as shown. Press away from four-patches.

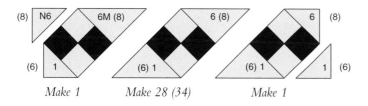

Make 1   *Make 28 (34)*   *Make 1*

2. Join all 30 (36) Four-Patch Unit 3's and half-square triangles N together for one side border. Press away from four-patches at both ends, press all other seams all in one direction. Repeat steps 1 and 2 for the three remaining side borders 1 and 3. Add the two side Pieced Borders 1 to the quilt. Set side Pieced Borders 3 aside.

3. For the top border, join the Four-Patch Unit 3's, two plain fabric square Unit 4's, and triangles M and N as described in step 1 and 2.

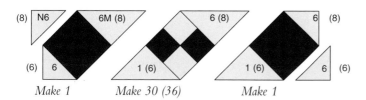

Make 1   *Make 30 (36)*   *Make 1*

Join all 30 (36) Four-Patch Unit 3's, two plain square Unit 4's, and half-square triangles N to complete the top border. Press away from plain squares at both ends. Press all other seams in one direction. Repeat for the bottom border. Add top and bottom Pieced Borders 1 to the quilt. Set top and bottom Pieced Borders 3 aside.

Pieced Border 2

Shape O: Cut three $1^5/_8$" × 40" strips from Fabric 4, sub-cut into sixty-eight $1^5/_8$" squares.

Shape P: Cut fourteen $3/_4$" × 40" strips from Fabric 3.

Shape Q: Cut seventeen $3/_4$" × 40" strips from Fabric 2.

Shape R: Cut 128 from Fabric 7, use Template R.

Shape S: Cut sixteen from Fabric 7, use Template S.

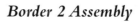

Unit 5, Make 68

Note: If you are not custom cutting Shape R and S from a border print type fabric, you can cut thirty-two $4^1/_4$" squares of chosen fabric and cut into quarters for Shape R. For Shape S, cut four $2^3/_8$" squares of chosen fabric and cut in half diagonally.

Border 2 Assembly

To make the sixty-eight individual OPQ Unit 5's, you will work in a Courthouse Steps style, meaning you will add to the Shape O square in a two sides, then top and bottom cadence.

1. Place one Shape O onto the Shape P Fabric 3 strip right sides together and sew as shown. Add the remaining sixty-seven Shape O's in similar fashion. Cut them apart, press seam away from O.

2. Place the sixty-eight OP Unit 5's onto the same Fabric 3 strip, aligning the opposite side of the unit to the strip edge and sew. Cut apart, press away from O.

3. Place the sixty-eight OPP Unit 5's onto the same Fabric 3 strip, aligning the top side of the unit to the strip edge and sew. Cut apart, press away from O.

4. Place the sixty-eight OPPP Unit 5's onto the same Fabric 3 strip, aligning the bottom side of the unit to the strip edge and sew. Cut apart, press away from O.

5. Place the sixty-eight OPPPP Unit 5's onto a Shape Q Fabric 2 strip and sew as before. Cut apart, press away from P.

6. Repeat Step 5 three more times, adding Shape Q Fabric 2 strip to the remaining three sides. A completed Unit 5 should measure $2^5/_8$" square as you hold it in your hand.

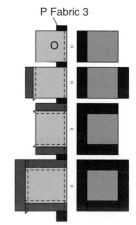

Side Border 2

Join sixteen Unit 5's with Shape R and S triangles as shown. Repeat once. Add the two side borders to the quilt.

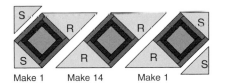

Make 1   Make 14   Make 1

Side Borders, make 2

Top and Bottom Border 2

Join eighteen Unit 5's with Shape R and S triangles as shown. Repeat once. Add to the top and bottom of the quilt.

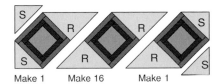

Make 1   Make 16   Make 1

Top and Bottom Borders, make 2

Pieced Border 3

Add to the sides, top and bottom of the quilt as you did for Pieced Border 1.

Final Multiple-Fabric Mitered Borders

1. Measure vertically and horizontally across the center of your quilt. Because this is a square quilt, the two numbers should be the same. If they are not, average them to get one number and write it down.

Cut four $3/4$" × 65" length grain strips of Fabric 2.

Cut four $3^1/2$" × 65" length grain strips of Fabric 3.

1. Join one Fabric 2 strip to one Fabric 3 strip four times.

2. Fold one strip unit in half to determine the center and place a pin. Measure in both directions from the center pin one half of the number you wrote down and place additional pins. Repeat for the remaining three border units. Now, pin each border unit to the quilt top, matching pins to the center and corners of the quilt top. Add additional pins as needed for smooth sewing and sew to the quilt top, starting and stopping $1/4$" from both corner pins and backstitch at both corners. Press stitches, press seam allowance to outside edge of the quilt. You will have a generous amount of overhang at both ends; do not cut anything off as you will need the extra fabric for mitering.

Border detail

Mitering the Borders by Hand

I miter borders by hand. To do this, take the quilt to the ironing board or a flat surface and work on one corner at a time. Position your work right side up and fold one border at a 45° angle over the opposite border that is extended out straight. Using a square ruler, continue to manipulate until the 45° angle line of the ruler is in alignment with the fold of the fabric at the corner, and the upper two edges of the ruler are in alignment with the two corresponding edges of the quilt. Press the fold, pin, then baste in place. Repeat for the remaining three corners. Trim the excess to $1/4$" from the fold after the four corners have been formed and evaluated. Hand appliqué the miters closed using a well-matched thread and small even stitches.

$1/4$" seam allowances included.

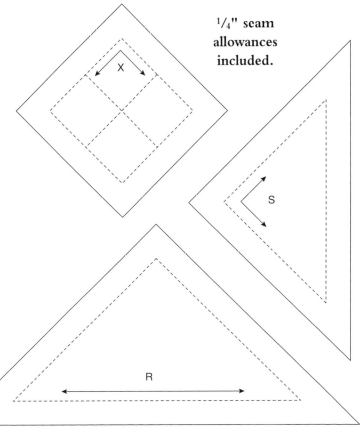

Gallery–
Ideas and Inspiration

A great way to use up all those practice blocks you've done! I used 3" blocks, added a very narrow border, page 45, and then a ¹/₂" wide final border. Use a larger print fabric for the back. Place a muslin square against both the back of the block and the wrong side of the backing to serve as a lining. Pipe the edge and fill with crushed walnut shells found at some pet stores…this is a great gift.

Medallion Sampler, *31" Square*

This award winning quilt satisfied my need to try a medallion-style quilt and my love of making sampler blocks. Surround your favorite 9" block with twelve 3" sampler blocks in the same set or try placing your block on square rather than on point.

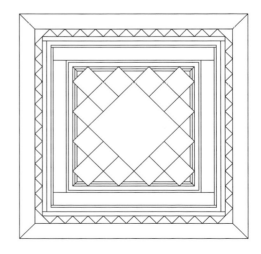

Captured Stars, *Framed 16" square*

This piece is a result of experimenting with fracturing the diamond shape of a 3" simple LeMoyne Star in four different ways, practicing Y-seam construction, and adding border detail.

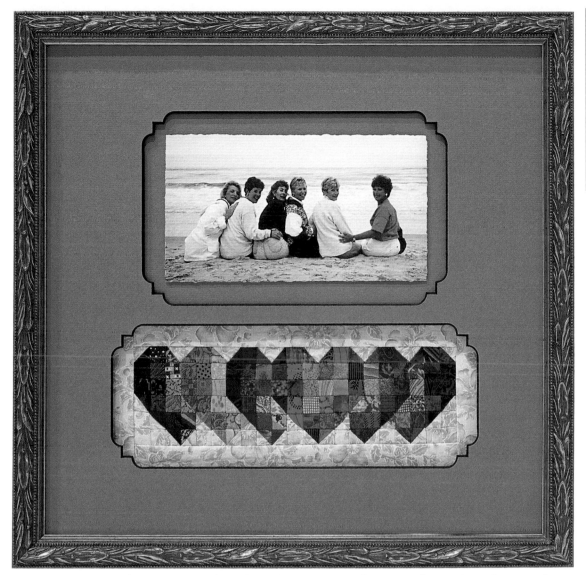

Heart to Heart, *Framed 13¹/₂" square. Left to right: Kathy McIntyre-Murphy, Peggy Gillette-Ogden, Sally Tear-Collins,
Pat Quick-Bowen, Kathy Tyler-Raubolt, Karen Johnson-Hart*

*This piece is dedicated to my five friends from grade school. We get together once a year to
laugh, cry, catch up, eat great food, and reminisce. I wanted to honor our special relationship
by combining a favorite photograph with patchwork. The Pieced Heart block was perfect. I
used the small block with a ³/₈" grid. It is constructed in horizontal rows and then the six
rows are joined. The color was the biggest challenge for me; a rough cut mock-up was a
must. Another idea might be to use a family photo with the hearts or perhaps a baby photo
combined with Tumbling Blocks—
page 81, or Jack-in-the-Box—page
65, or a photo of you and your
Gramma with Grandmother's
Flower Garden—page 82.*

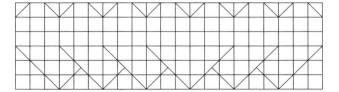

Autumn Window, *framed 24" × 17"*

My challenge here was to combine two sizes of trees (6" and 4") and use a new color palette. It is designed on a ¹/₄" grid on point. The 6" tree units are ³/₄" and the 4" tree units are ¹/₂". The 6" tree also has additional smaller leaves that create more detail and an opportunity to add hot color in small amounts. The darkened lines on the schematic indicate the piecing sections, the X indicates the partial seaming areas of the tree.

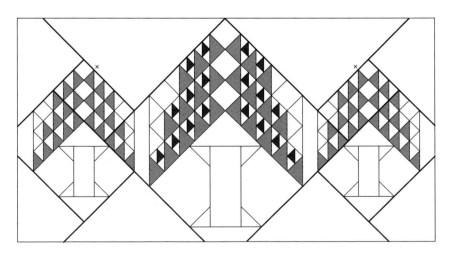

Flamenco, *22" Square*

*This piece combines my block, Double Ohio Star in the 6"
size, set on point, with Baby Bunting units to create a
unique inner border design detail. Adding the curved piped
edge enhances and reinforces the curvy feeling in the patchwork. My challenge was to use a variety of visual textures in
a limited color palette. The baby bunting idea could be adapt-
ed to a variety of different blocks…what's your favorite?*

Postage Stamp Keepsake, *framed 17¹/₂" × 13"*

This keepsake celebrates the Postage Stamp Basket block actually becoming a thirteen cent stamp in March, 1978. The actual stamps are still available, just look in the yellow pages under stamp collectors. I tried to choose fabrics that "felt" like the actual stamp.

Gizmo, 16¹/₂" *square*

This quilt was designed on a 1" grid and is constructed in sections, not whole blocks. The size of the Churn Dash blocks are 3", 4¹/₂", and 1¹/₂". The darkened lines indicate the sections that are sewn and then joined. This is simple sewing so make your challenge color! I chose the background as a palette fabric and then pulled all my block fabrics from it, as described on pages 11–12.

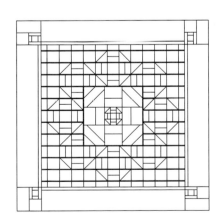

Basket

Add ¹⁄₄" seam allowances to each pattern.

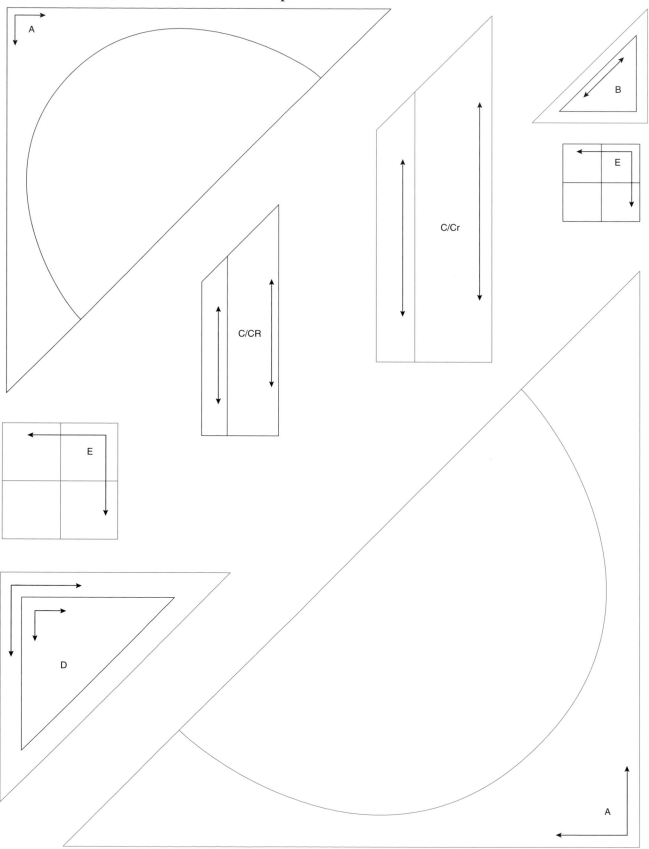

A

B

C/Cr

E

C/CR

E

D

A

Interlocking Squares

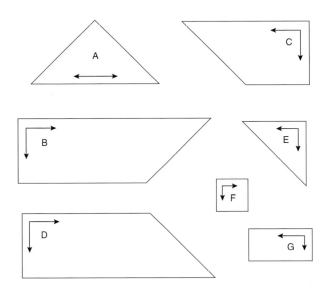

Postage Stamp Basket

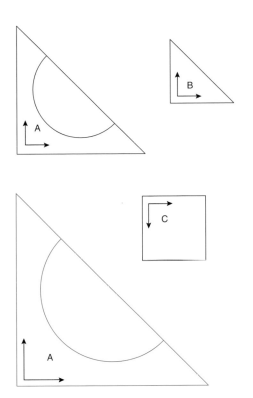

Log Cabin

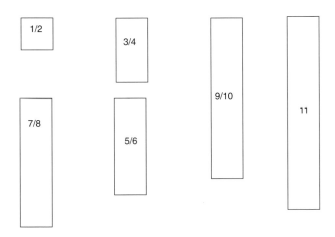

Tumbling Block

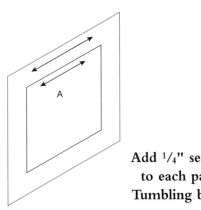

**Add ¼" seam allowances
to each pattern except
Tumbling block patterns.**

Bear's Paw

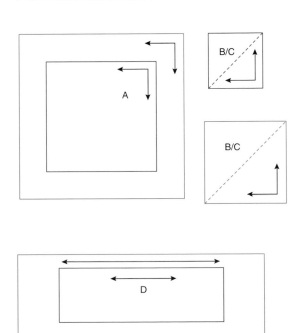

House

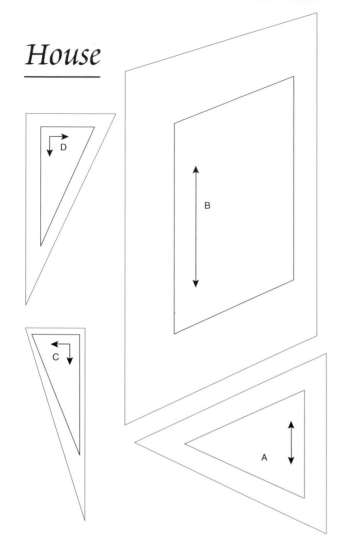

D

B

C

A

Vagabond

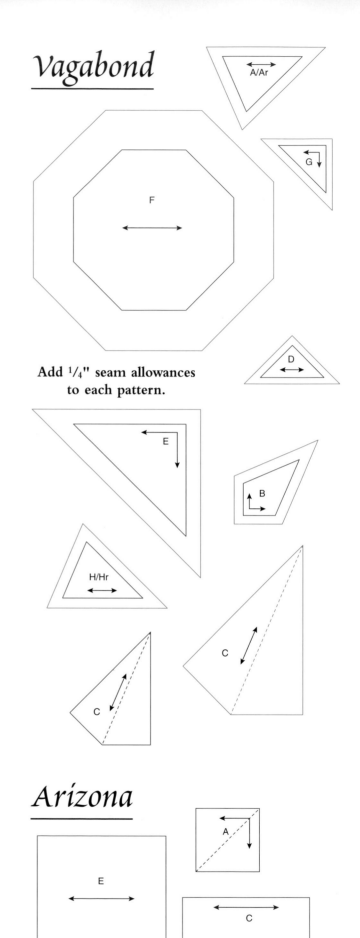

A/Ar

G

F

D

Add ¹/₄" seam allowances to each pattern.

E

B

H/Hr

C

C

California Sunset Variation

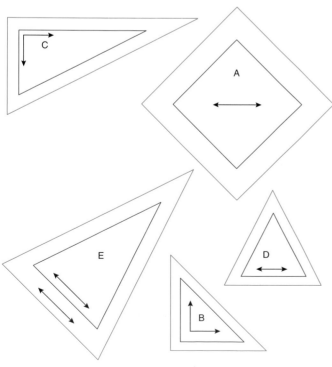

C

A

E

D

B

Arizona

A

E

C

Sunbonnet Sue and Overall Bill

Ten Pointed Star

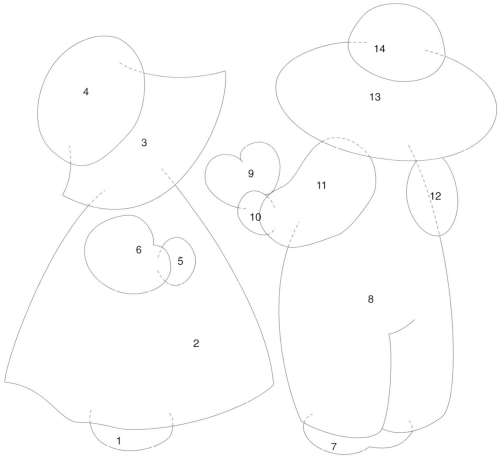

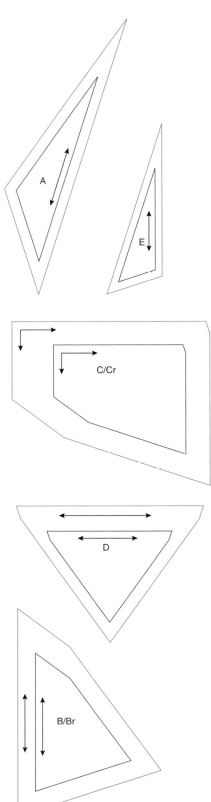

Add ¼" seam allowances to each pattern except for
Sunbonnet Sue and Overall Bill.

Carnival Ride

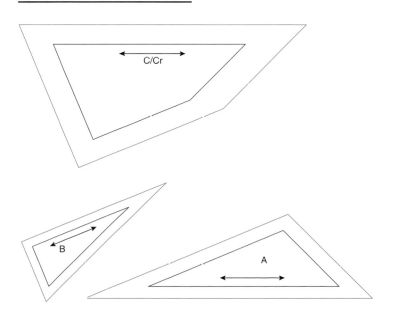

Cornucopia

Castle Wall

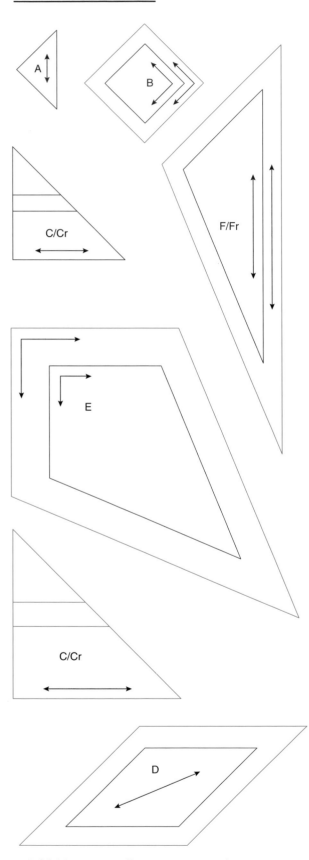

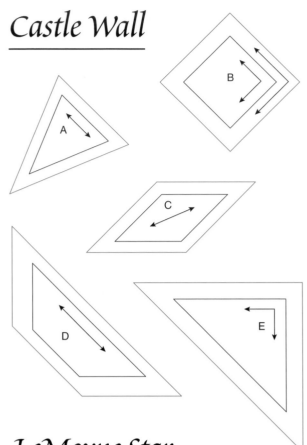

LeMoyne Star, Morning Star, Split-Diamond LeMoyne Star

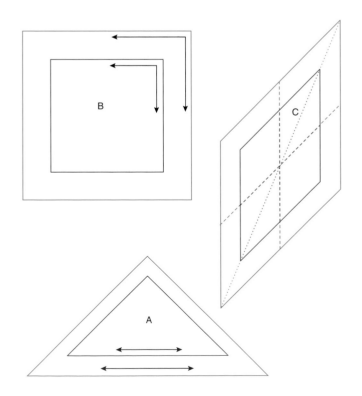

Add ¼" seam allowances to each pattern.

Five Pointed Star

Tall Ship

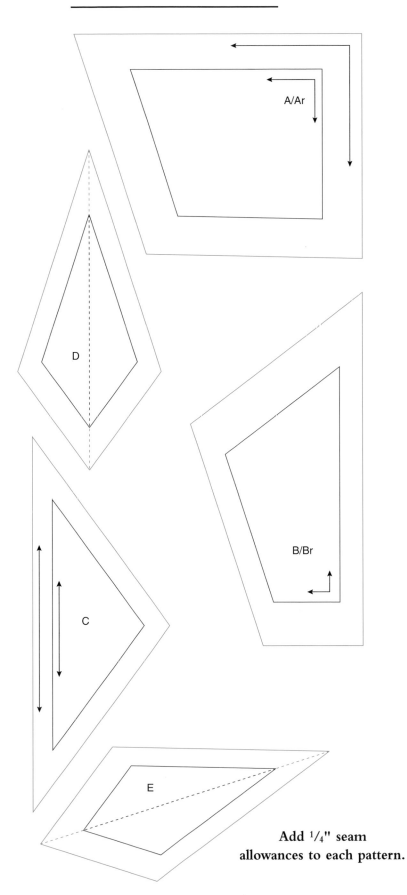

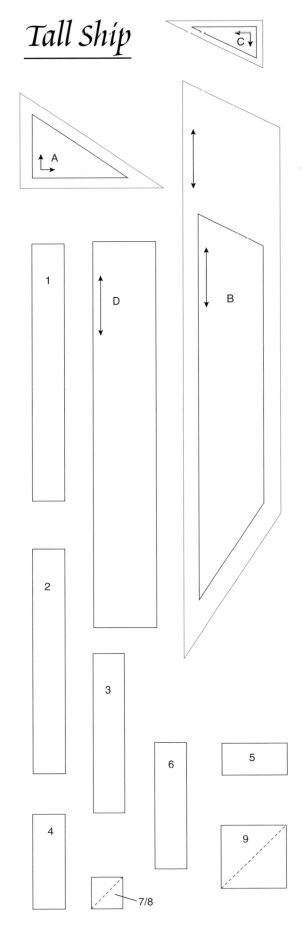

Add 1/4" seam allowances to each pattern.

North Carolina Lily

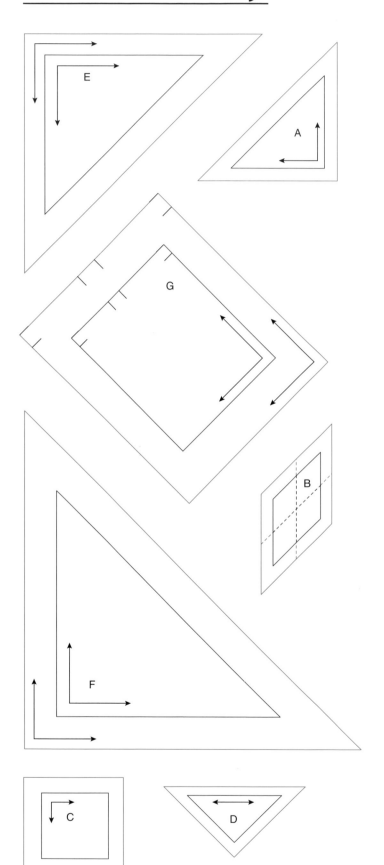

Charleston Quilt

Add ¼" seam allowances to each pattern except for Leaf Design.

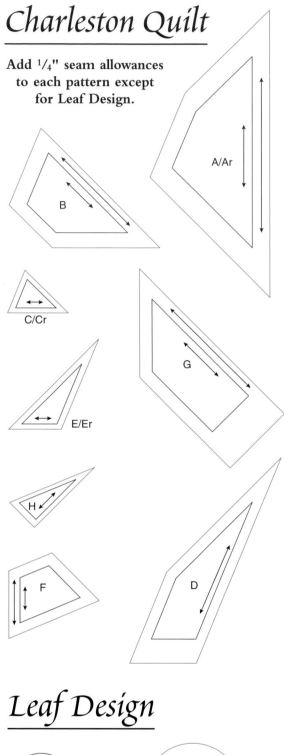

Leaf Design

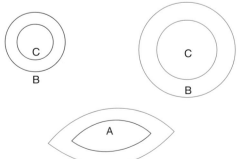

Bibliography

Beyer, Jinny. *Patchwork Patterns*, EPM Publications, Virginia, 1979

Beyer, Jinny. *The Quilters Album of Blocks and Borders*, EPM Publications, Virginia, 1980

Barnes, Christine. *Color: The Quilters Guide*, That Patchwork Place, Washington, 1997

Collins, Sally. *Small Scale Quiltmaking*, C&T Publishing, California, 1996

Johnson-Srebro, Nancy. *Rotary Magic*, Rodale Press, Pennsylvania, 1998

McCloskey, Marsha. *Lessons in Machine Piecing*, That Patchwork Place, Washington, 1990

Perry, Gai. *Color From The Heart*, C&T Publishing, California, 1999

Squier-Craig, Sharyn. *Drafting Plus*, Chitra Publications, Pennsylvania, 1994

Wolfrom, Joen. *The Magical Effects of Color*, C&T Publishing, California, 1992.

Sources

$1/_{16}$" Hole Punch

The Cotton Club
P.O. Box 2263
Boise, Idaho 83701
Phone: 208-345-5567
FAX: 208-345-1217
Email: cotton@micron.net
WWW: http://www.cottonclub.com

Graph Paper

Chitra Publications
Public Avenue
Montrose, Pennsylvania 18801
Phone: 800-628-8244
Chitrapix@epic.net

Quilting Supplies

Cotton Patch Mail Order
3405 Brown Avenue, Dept. CTB
Lafayette, CA 94549
Phone: 800-835-4418
Phone: 925-283-7883
e-mail: quiltusa@yahoo.com
http://www.quiltusa.com

Index

About the Author

Sally Collins grew up in Trenton, Michigan, and moved to California in 1975. She took her first quilting class in 1978 and discovered the pleasure of the art. Her immediate and continual love and interest is in the process of quiltmaking, the journey. She loves the challenge of combining quality workmanship, small intricate piecing and traditional blocks. Through this book she hopes to introduce quilters to her perspective on quiltmaking as she shares her methods and techniques to help quiltmakers critique and correct their own work, improve their technical and creative skills and find joy in the process.

Sally spends her time traveling across the country sharing quilts, teaching workshops, and enjoying life with her husband Joe, son Sean, daughter-in-law Evelyn and grandchildren, Kaylin and Joey. Workshop and lecture inquires may be sent directly to Sally Collins at 1640 Fieldgate Lane, Walnut Creek, California, 94595.

Another book by Sally Collins

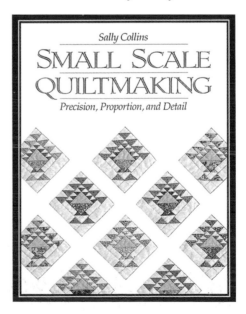

Other Fine Books From C&T Publishing:

For more information write for a free catalog:
C&T Publishing, Inc.
P.O. Box 1456, Lafayette, CA 94549
(800) 284-1114
e-mail: ctinfo@ctpub.com
Website: www.ctpub.com